# ANTI CLI MAX

A PERSONAL
ESSAY ON DESIRE,
AND THE LACK OF IT

# ANTI CLI MAX

A PERSONAL
ESSAY ON DESIRE,
AND THE LACK OF IT
BY **MATEO
SANCHO
CARDIEL**

"Anticlimax" by Mateo Sancho Cardiel.
New York, 2017.
Illustrated by Irene Alós Sancho.
Translated by Tom Bunstead
ISBN 9781520658315

# INDEX

Thanks for staying, Nelson
Thanks for listening, Clara
Thanks for everything, mamá y papá

"Do not ask who I am
and do not ask me to remain the same"
Michel Foucault

# COFFEE AND SEX

"To me," I said to my friend Clara, "having sex is like making coffee. Since I don't enjoy the end product, I can never tell if it's actually any good." After years of going over and over the same subject, in one of the aleatory, almost Dadaist phone conversations we have before bed to purge our minds of the day, finally, here was something that felt accurate, concrete. We'd been going over things we'd already discussed a million times, a bit like the way you watch your favourite movie time and again. But then this epiphanylike thing, this unexpected bringing together in a single image of something that's plagued me for years. My penance. Goddamn sex.

I'm forever being asked: "how did you manage to not become a coffee addict living in Italy?" People also find it surprising, because I'm quite an energetic person, that I don't drink coffee. I suppose it might be odd for someone not to like coffee, and though when I initially gave it up I thought people wouldn't care, I get these questions so much my reaction has evolved to a not-reaction; I smile, offer nothing in the way of explanation, and possibly come across as grasping for some kind of ambiguous halo. I imagine people might think I'm a recovering caffeine fiend, though I never correct the assumption if it is there.

But I do still partake in coffee as something to tackle the entropy of the everyday. For example, a house, to me, isn't complete without some kind of coffee maker. Whatever the reason, Good Host Syndrome maybe, I always keep coffee in the kitchen for guests;

I know only too well that normal people like coffee first thing in the morning or after a meal. I'm in my twenties, and though I see many of my generation as being massively complacent, there are also those of us who are very complaisant – amenable, giving.

Whenever I'm obliged to, I make coffee as best I can. I learned the art of making coffee in Italy and my view is that using Nespresso takes all the charm out of a process whose culmination I may not enjoy but can still admire from afar. I like the smell, I like watching coffee lovers enjoying it, I even quite like the way the grounds can be used to unblock drains. It's a ritual that's ingrained in our culture. So it's within me though I'm merely a spectator; it's familiar to me in spite of the sensory distance.

Inevitably, from this outside perspective, there's a margin for error, which the person I've made the coffee for might fill with pretence, saying the coffee's lovely when really it tastes like mud. In the ensuing minutes, doubt rears its head. In the previous, the worry that I unwittingly skipped an important part of the process. And then, as the caffeine's hitting the drinker, I'll probably be a little worn out by the whole thing and ready for a snooze.

I don't like espressos, lattes, cappuccinos, Irish coffees or our Spanish carajillos, which are made with brandy and lemon peel. To me, coffee's coffee. Only if it comes with a good dollop of mascarpone on top, and only if it's been through a long process of soaking side by side with sponge biscuits, can I forget that it's there; I'm a big fan of tiramisu, because it's a recipe that needs a lot of time and care to make; it's no good, for example, unless you leave it to chill properly. But there's nothing medical or moral in my opposition to coffee. I have no problem with it on a concept level, I see how effective it is to stop you falling asleep in front of the computer or at the wheel, it never kept me up at night when I did used to drink it, and I don't see it as particularly unhealthy, either; I just don't like the taste. I simply don't like it, I don't tend to feel any need for it, and my body has learned to regulate itself without.

Coffee substitutes – Coke, tea, hot chocolate – don't interest me. But, pulled along by what you might call the vagaries of linguistic usage, I sometimes join my workmates for a midmorning "coffee break". Though I only ever have orange juice, I get really into the discussion panel initiated around cups that, one way or another, always end up staining the tablecloth. I've even surprised myself from time to time by suggesting to someone, with obvious ulterior motives, "let's go for coffee". I've even been known, since giving up, to drink a cup, just so as not to make a scene.

But there are some differences between sex and coffee. If you abstain from the latter, no one's going to jump to the conclusion that your dad must have tipped scalding hot coffee on you as a child (like Gloria Grahame in Fritz Lang's The Big Heat), or that you've witnessed destitute Colombians being whipped and worked half to death on a plantation. So much as mention that sex isn't your thing, and words like repression spring straight into people's minds, trauma, priggishness, whether or not they choose to tell you. I'm not saying there's no explanation for it, that there mightn't be some well spring to the psychological river flowing out into this sea of not-desire. But the pressure to keep up normal societal habits is there, and it's huge. At best, it makes people look at you with unbearable compassion; at worst, like they're worried you might leap up and bite them.

"There's nothing that everyone likes" is a Spanish phrase I return to, or take refuge in, when I'm trying to explain all this. If nothing, absolutely nothing, is to everyone's liking, why on earth should sex be an exception? But the thing that can really get to you when you try to tell people you don't find sex particularly enjoyable, but honestly not traumatic either, is the immediate moral or psychiatric conclusions they jump to; why shouldn't I be allowed to abstain in peace, why can't I just say it isn't my number one priority? It feels like there's a collective opposition, a psychoanalytic front, almost, and it's arrayed against anything of the sort. If you don't eat, you die. If you don't fuck or aren't interested in fucking, same kind of thing, supposedly. Am I Bruce Willis in The Sixth Sense then? Read on, just in case!

The real let down feels like the fact that, for all the advances there have been in terms of individual freedoms, it sometimes seems like choice has been displaced rather than increased. Another way of putting it is that I feel like a happily installed housewife during a phase when women are clamouring to join the workforce. A traitor to some cause. If I find fulfilment baking cakes and looking after the kiddies, and hate the idea of making power plays in executive boardrooms, what do I do then? There are so many options nowadays, queer, straight, bi, transsexual, everything in between – I'm missing out plenty, but it's hard not to get lost in that particular everything in between – but why isn't lack of appetite counted among them? Not even necessarily as an official orientation, but at least as an option. I don't particularly want my feelings analyzed and understood, but respected as a personal choice, yes.

If the idea of the housewife is automatically associated with centuries of female subjection, the idea of not loving sex is put in a box just as quickly with ideas about fustiness, complexes, moral corsetry. The only available archetype for people who don't love sex is very difficult to identify with: they must be repressed homosexuals, or victims of childhood abuse, emotionally blocked, allergic to washing themselves, loners, or simply uneasy on the eye... Sex fled them, rather than the other way round; they were made asexual by some ghastly process of elimination. Nothing could be further from the truth! I wouldn't say I'm a stunner, but neither am I repulsive. There's a Spanish phrase that translates literally as: "God gives bread to those who have no teeth"; I'd say this is what genuinely unattractive people would think of me, in that, I don't lack propositions, but I never take them. Good-looking people would say, again translating literally: "More was lost in the war" – that is, in this case, relatively, nothing is lost. Life goes on. And I don't think I'm overstating it if I say I never have problems pulling. Strangely, this has been even more the case since I began to say to myself I don't need to make an effort to be like everyone else. Life's little ironies, I suppose, or reverse psychology maybe.

But I've found out that this condition (if I can call it that) has even taken backward steps. People didn't used to constantly try to work out the underlying reasons for absolutely everything, but nowadays even the least provocative of attitudes has become a taboo to be dismantled and understood. My mindset is called old-fashioned now, people like me are called crocked, or, worse, we're some sort of aberration, a disaster that has to be looked into. The contradictions of progress.

"You do have a problem," said my friend Nieves, "but you just don't experience it as such." Nieves is someone whose intellect is strictly artistic, she has this amazing capacity to abstract from the practicalities of life. Whether that's good or bad… For the millionth time in the three months since she moved in with me after breaking up with her boyfriend, we were looking for an answer to the question. Me chipping in on the emotion side, her in terms of instincts.

"You don't have a problem, or at least nothing you can't manage yourself" was the phrase that prompted me to stop seeing the sex counsellor I went to as a student – when I was still trying to reconcile myself with the crowd. I won't deny it, this feeling of having to fit in has been the one thing that's made me believe sex is the true axis on which everything turns...

Another view, held by some of the less helpful people I've spoken to, is: "Women have felt exactly the same for centuries, and they've never complained." My brother, who himself manages to shrewdly integrate his intelligence and his baser instincts, is of the view that: "To not like sex, you must be really fucked. " And a corollary to this is the mother's view – Mum knows best! – which is: "I just think it's that you're an angel," said mine when I let her in on this conflict... and then asked her to pay for the sex counsellor.

I'll try to respond to these assertions one by one.

Problem? If this were a "manifesto," I wouldn't dare call it that. "A problem" in medical terms will only become a pathology, and we don't want that. But, as with any minority, without being inherently problematic, they always end up becoming thorny and difficult to solve. Being on the side of asexuality is a problem not in terms of social acceptance – after all, it's something deeply personal – but it is certainly an obstacle in the subconscious race we're all involved in, some more that others, maybe, the finishing line being to find your significant other. For a long time

I was clear about this being a basic aspiration in everyone's life, and in a way it saddens me now how many doubts I have about the idea. Some part of my subconscious has discarded the possibility altogether; on the other hand, it has always seemed like a kind of miracle for the stars to cross and the love be requited, for there to be the physical impulse as well as for the personalities to be compatible, and for the two people to meet at a time in their lives when they both want to commit… It's rare. But, on top of that, to expect that the person you like so much understands that you aren't into sex and a) accepts it and b) doesn't let it effect their own self esteem – then we're heading into triple corkscrew and a double tummy tuck territory.

Can I manage it myself? Yes, luckily. Or at least I can at the moment, buoyed up by the very stimulating life I live.

The sex counselor at my University, whose surgery I'd travel to after lectures once a week, carried out some tests on me, checking whether I had problems sleeping, or if food made me anxious, or if I cried myself to sleep at night for no apparent reason. She struck off frustration and obsessive tendencies straight away. But, just in case, she gave me some strange behavioral exercises as "homework"; first, she gave me a small rubber truncheon to hit myself with any time I had a negative thought, and, secondly, she told me to make lists of things I had memorized (multiplication tables, people's birthdays, etc) and to wheel them out to counter the fatalistic thoughts that arose any time I got into a sexual situation. I went with what I'd learned best as a child and the thing that still serves me in my work as a writer on cinema: Oscar winners, year by year. The erotic scenes began to come thick and fast, then, to the beat of my memorized facts: "1941: How Green Was My Valley; 1942: Mrs. Miniver; 1943: Casablanca..."

The sex counselor quickly came to the conclusion that sex was only one of the areas affected by what was in fact my core issue: assertiveness. That is, doing things when I really want to do them, and not at all if I don't want to. What she didn't expect – and in fact, she didn't find out, because I never managed to bring myself to say it – is that sex, as generally understood, is something I simply hardly ever feel like doing. And if I do do it (when I told my parents this, they looked at me like I'm E.T.), most of the time it's only because I see no way of avoiding it. Sometimes I manage to get out of it, but usually not. I must be among the very few people who have more sex than they'd like. I'm sexually harassed!

Am I so unusual? If I'm like this "by birth", obviously it's going to seem normal to me, but anyone I tell still finds it very far from normal. This might be because I still find it difficult to explain the thing clearly, and straight away I get into a muddle. Which is what this book is born out of, really. Virginia Woolf said in The Waves that we tell stories to make sense of our own lives. Stories that clarify our stories. Following this, I'm going to see whether, by taking this confused concept to pieces, I can explain and at the same time understand for myself all the contradictions related to a way of being that keeps me at a distance from most people. And it's precisely this search that my brother (whose inclination is always not to overthink) says qualifies me as the fucked up sexless me.

That women have suffered the same thing, except in silence? On the one hand, that hardly seems like a reason to keep the flame alive, even if Winston Churchill was right in defining success as the ability to go from one defeat to another with no loss of enthusiasm. Maybe I just have to assume that my natural habitat is not the hormonedriven world. But, on the other hand, there are surely large numbers of women who haven't enjoyed sex purely because their partners haven't made it enjoyable for them, or because they haven't been sufficiently sexually cultured to demand what gives them pleasure. If there's one thing I don't want to do with this discourse it's to put people who don't achieve a full sexual life in the same box as those who are sexually disinclined; process against starting point, as it were. I'd share with these women – and very likely with many men too – the challenge of demanding what I want in sex. In my case, it would be to find a way of saying that my libido has a much lower limit than I would ideally like. It isn't that I don't have any desire, it's just that it's sated very quickly. My mother says that ever since I was young my appetite would vanish just seeing the food on the plate, and it feels something like that with sex too… But to go back to these women, the vast majority of those who say sex isn't their cup of tea (especially older woman), I think that their problem really lies in finding a way of saying how – and with whom – they want to do it.

Finally, my mother's not very orthodox vision of me as an angel which, though it might seem naïve to say so, seems to strike closest to the nature of my reality for many years – if we understand reality, that is, as each individual's sense of the world – and the certainty that, for me, sex, this titanic (and tyrannical) force, is no great shakes. I can take it or leave it. This undermines the fact that it's such a fundamental motivation for so many people, it makes it seem somewhat unreal – like angels. That so much history has been written in the bedchamber, that so many religions have felt the need to control this aspect of human behaviour if they are to control the human overall. That, ultimately, so many people (of both sexes) "think with their dicks". These impulses don't affect me, and at the same time, for the exact same reason, I feel very vulnerable to them. On top of this, the chocolate sprinkles on the frothy cappuccino of my membership of minority groups, as it were, is that within my asexuality, my leaning is toward being gay. If I have to choose, I go for sexual partners of the same sex. You don't like chocolate sprinkles? Here, have some more!

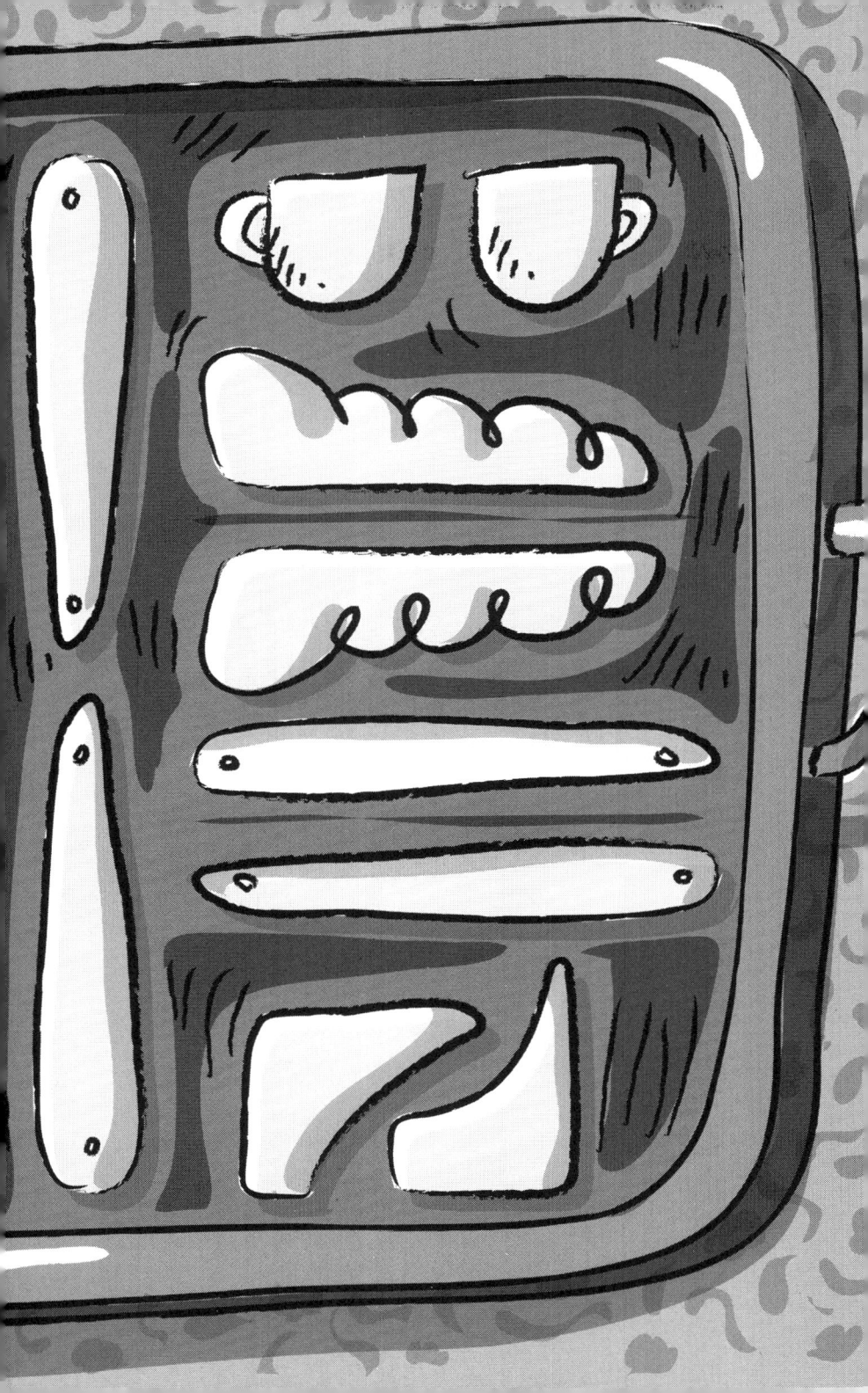

# OUTING: TAKE 2?

There are some things that, once you do them you think they're for life. Things that it's better to do sooner rather than later, so you can move forward. This was my reasoning for getting braces on my teeth but as it turned out I was wrong; having suffered them as a kid, a year of ulcers, brackets, not being able to talk normally, more brackets, and, of course, the unavoidable aesthetic issues associated with large amount of metal in your oral cavity, I then had to go back to the orthodontist twelve years later because the problem was worse than it had initially seemed. I had to put up with the contraption for another two and a half years and needed an operation on my jaw. Maxillofacial Osteotomy, the operation's called. An innovative technique, invasive and not very well known, but, don't worry, once it's over, you'll see, you'll look fantastic.

Once again, the metaphor applies. In this second potential outing the rules also change somewhat. No need to operate, let's keep panic to a minimum. But here I begin into a less well trod field, one that will leave aside all that is plain and obvious and require deep work – a less explored, pioneer path. "Asexuality" might seem the most appropriate label for what I've been talking about but, following lengthy research, the lack of precision as well as the complexities associated with this referent make me extremely wary of using it.

In comparison, the prejudices you find against homosexuality are few. And the asexual community hasn't even formulated a self-justifying body of pamphlets and manifestos yet. I'm not even sure about the idea of calling it a collective at all, it makes me feel a bit allergic, partly because any advances have been glacial – not just slow, but with important damage at the edges of its forward movement, and traces of sediment that move backwards rather than advancing. Sediment, deposits, that is, consisting of the people who feel marginalized within a minority that is trying to gain political momentum. And theirs is an unspoken abandonment, a bitter feeling like having taken a beating, of having been rejected by all and sundry. Something akin to the treatment of Herta Müller and the Swabians in Romania, who were slammed by the Nazis in Germany and then, because of their Germanic blood, accused of being Nazis by the Communists.

Though not quite so dramatically, I've always felt a related sense of being "residual" myself with respect to the gay movement. On holiday in Stockholm once, I wasn't let in to a gay bar. I asked myself, what kind of accreditation might I show? A feather boa, possibly... Don't I look trendy enough? Eyebrows too bushy? I feel like I have little to do with the movement's most visible elements, to the point where sometimes I even feel excluded by them because, unfortunately, the most shrill are often the ones who also fail to listen. Although I won't deny I've jumped on the rainbow bandwagon from time to time, I'm no stranger to a little hedonism, but now I've decided to go my own way. Really, the question I'm trying to answer here comes down to a simple old who am I? And, accepting that my argument mightn't, overall, add up, I'd rather not try and take on a whole movement if at the same time I'm going to be laying bare my weaknesses, my contradictions and fears.

Being a teenager at the end of the twentieth century, the internet was an important aid in discovering that I was gay. A voyage of discovery in the classical sense: a little bit of information, purely theoretical, conversing with gays in different parts of the world (chats in English are curious because your linguistic imperfections actually mean you come more quickly to the nub) and, why not, some porn – men on men wasn't such an easy thing to find at the local cinema or on the five TV channels that made up the cultural universe of the small Pyrenean town I lived in at the time. Aside from porn, in which I obviously didn't see bodies I recognized as similar to mine, I did find online a certain amount of pretty bog standard discourse I did see myself reflected in. And stumbling upon this, and the effect it had on me, made me realize that I'd felt alone for a long time but hadn't known it, and I felt a kind of refuge in the awareness that I wasn't the only one on this tangent. Years later I was on a date and my 'partenaire' told me about a theory to do with the link between Spain opening up to the gay community and the internet becoming faster and cheaper: the fact we could spend long periods of time in chatrooms made "Spanish poofs" aware of how numerous they were and their potential force as a collective. I don't know if it could be proved, but there's little doubt that the Millennium bug, far from bringing down the world's computers, saw hordes of us, out of the closet and on the streets – at least in Barcelona and Madrid. The twenty first century was looking promising.

My theory, which isn't based very much on evidence but I find interesting nonetheless, has more to do with commerce, and I came up with it after spending time in Rome on an Erasmus study year in 2004-5, which was also when Pope John Paul II died. Whereas in Italy men's fashion was a multi million Euro industry, in good ol' macho Spain, where women were still laying out men's' clothes for them in the morning, people were still coming to terms with the only section of society who bought these products: the gays. Out of this essentially commercial interest, acceptance was fostered, as in Spain we become accustomed to things if we see them on TV and, little by little, gays had started appearing on our screens. Around this time, homosexuality was also glamorized in other ways. And then you get the domino effect of metrosexuals, men plucking their eyebrows to look like Audrey Hepburn, studs with shaved chests and legs...

In any case, whatever it was, the dawn of a new century, the internet, Madonna, when I came out it was actually fairly painless. First there was the parental hurdle, which was the most important one for me and saw a few tears, but after that everything was pretty fluid. I was pleased to see how, first in New York and Berlin, and later in Madrid, homosexuality began to develop real variety, just as much as heterosexuality. Plus the fact gays are all sensitive, good looking, intellectual, creative... As if!

But yes, if the gay movement came into the world already mature and grounded, which is something to be grateful for (although this is skipping certain important things, especially the question of leaving children behind), in its asexual counterpart everything's still pretty undeveloped and I'm not entirely convinced it will end up as a movement at all. Everything's still too "unwashed" or, at least, the referent "asexual" lacks precision: for a start, the negatory a seems to me too strong. I have the feeling that, though I was lucky about the point in history when I came out, now I'm going to have to play out of my skin as I embark on this path, almost pioneer-like. All in aid of the possibility that one day, people's minds will be ready to meet someone who admits to not loving sex that much – so people won't automatically run a mile.

As a student, firstly in my hometown and then in Madrid taking a not very demanding course in journalism, I had all the time in the world to dedicate to self-discovery and exploration – both virtual and real. Now I'm working in this at times thankless profession, my time is less but my weapons have multiplied. In my area of journalism, culture, my approach has always been rhetorical rather than investigative, but I did manage to find a professional excuse to air my hypotheses on asexuality. Chosen moment: Valentine's Day. Concept: if the idea of sex without love has raced ahead, where has that left the idea of love without sex? In the process, I found out that the internet also has its small space for asexuals, and it turned my stomach. Flashback to my hometown and, once more, a window on the world. I felt what it was like again to be amongst people so different to me, for all the thousands of caveats this long-ago feeling contained. I shed a tear inside. And felt the angst again of having to redefine who I was. There's always a lot of talk of the majority's prejudices against minorities, but I've always thought it worse the way these prejudices form part of the make up of these minorities and how they have to sort through them, one after another, to find the truth about themselves. If a person doesn't know his or her place, they don't know to cling on to themselves. And in this case, asexual is an awful category; very forceful, very excluding. Going through all the various subcategories – which, as anywhere, contain all kinds of imbeciles – I really did find horns for my shoes and I also rediscovered a fundamental reality that I sometimes forget when thinking about myself: as people, we're so changeable and fluid as a species that to label ourselves, while it may be good for stability, doesn't help us to progress as individuals. But, exactly for this reason, and ever since I began discussing the subject in my circle of close friends, I felt that the "asexual" question, understood as an ongoing condition but also something that occurs in one single moment, concerns many more people than it seems.

For my article I interviewed Anthony Bogaert, a professor in the Psychology Department at Brock University, Ottawa, who had carried out a poll with a random sample of 1,800 people from England. The study based on the results was published in 2004. Buried beneath questions on precautions to prevent AIDS, it registered that 1% of the respondents "didn't feel attracted either by people of their own or the opposite sex", although if the 30% of respondents who preferred not to answer this question had been included, the proportion of asexuals would presumably have been higher.

In accordance with good scientific practice, Professor Bogaert looked at the study to try and find other factors that coincided with asexuality: age, social standing, education... The obvious, with obvious results. But two years later, though I don't know what it was that changed his perspective and led to the eureka moment, Bogaert reassessed his studies, now declaring himself open to the possibility that these respondents showed not an absence of desire, but simply a less strong desire. "It doesn't necessarily mean that these individuals have no desire for sexual stimulation, rather that the majority have a lower interest in it," he said in summery. For me, there's the rub: the question of "interest". It isn't rejection, it isn't aversion. It's disinterest.

Dr Bogaert therefore discarded the idea of asexuality as a fourth sexuality option, seeing it rather as an option that everyone might apply to their chosen sexuality. Which, as must already be clear, fitted my situation like a glove. So, distinguishing asexuality from Hypoactive Sexual Desire Desorder (HSDD), he pointed to "one important difference: asexuals still have a certain amount of desire, excitement or sexual activity, and they might even find some pleasure in these. Nonetheless, they simply don't connect or direct any of these things with or toward any person or thing." And Bogaert also recognized that, even in the case of those with HSDD, "there exists a significant number of people with a longstanding absence of sexual desire who have never been diagnosed with HSDD because they're perfectly happy and/or they function adequately in their interpersonal relations". In summary: "If you are defined as asexual it doesn't necessarily mean that you are suffering or that the condition in any way interferes in your interpersonal functioning." Great: the good thing about scientists, unlike journalists, is their lack of sensationalism.

In my case, writing this article was not so much sensational as altogether revelatory.

Within the things that asexuality might mean – another part of the report dealt with couples who stayed together, stoically, in spite of the loss of sexual interest – a whole series of doors opened in me that, in turn, opened another infinity of doubts in terms of my identity. Round and round we go!

Starting with the anecdotal, the funniest thing was to discover this movement that, in its most extreme manifestation – which also refuses sentimentality – had spawned t-shirts eulogizing "amoeba lifestyle" as a kind of total freedom. Also the fact that figures as well known as Dali, Chopin and England's Elizabeth I (not for nothing known as the Virgin Queen) were claimed by the collective to swell their ranks as celebrated participants.

Moving on to less comfortable things, I spoke with certain psychoanalysts whose view was that asexuality was an impossibility. In their view, sexuality is, by default, sexuality, and, quite aside from coitus, fellatio, whatever you want to call it – getting off – inherent in human beings. At first I railed against this, but then I'm afraid that through the writing of this book I've had to submit to some of their postulations. Not to the extent that I agree that even when we're making spaghetti we're having sex in a veiled way, or that every single disorder originates in some sexual conflict – on that front I'm more with Jung than Freud – but, yes, in trying to understand my lack of desire, I've actually come to see that many of my supposedly cauterized conflicts do in fact contain heat – the heat of sex.

But for me the most important thing in my research, quite aside from what might lead someone to the point of not feeling desire, was finding that, although few and far between, there were indeed examples of asexuals who had achieved that high wire act of nonetheless developing emotionally. In September of 2008, there was an article in the British newspaper The Guardian on a young man named Paul Cox who, after 24 years of asexuality, got married. This in spite of the fact Professor Bogaert said that "the asexual finds it very difficult to find a partner, and this is an indubitable source of stress." Ooh, ah, so stressful! And how might Mr. and Mrs. Cox be now?

I soon came across sites like Platonic Partners, a contact site for loving encounters free of the yoke of sex. I made myself a profile but didn't then see anything, frankly, that interested me. I also surfed my way to Ace of Hearts, a blog written by an asexual woman – who was recently and happily married and who also found excitement in her relationship – sealed the deal. But my most significant find was the page of the Asexual Visibility and Education Network (AVEN) that, though it set down asexuality as a sexual option (which I don't go along with) was nonetheless super interesting, chock full of testimonies – generally not very promising in terms of my future emotional life, with discussion threads such as: "Am I condemned to being alone?" and "Can I fake it, even a little bit?" and with a lot of other well-researched pieces. The forums are passionately argued and give the impression of a well organized collective, although there's also a lot of religious nonsense and comments that argue for a supposed "asexual superiority" based on the idea that being led by your hormones is a waste of important energies. Nonetheless, when I was at Gay Pride in San Francisco in 2010, I saw people from AVEN marching, and though at first I was encouraged to see they had a presence, in the end there was something about the way they presented themselves that felt very distancing to me. I couldn't identify with them at all. I suppose all beginnings are complicated, and I'm not someone who judges people based purely on whether or not they look like Apollo (which is how the gay movement seems sometimes) but this little troupe were... a bit all over the place, if I can put it like that. In opposing heteronorms, they went further – apart from anything, taking themselves so seriously in a festival context – than I felt comfortable with. And they didn't do much for the "don't look at us, join us" idea, which is what any self-respecting march surely needs to get across.

What most made me feel distant from them was that I don't believe love to be any less distracting than sex or, in any case, that this whole headache about asexuality, or this lack-of-appetite posture, are in any way easy to comprehend. I believe it to have been the principal destabilizing factor in my life. So, just as happened with me and homosexuality, I've refused to enter into the complacent attitude that considers asexuality a kind of more intellectually acute worldview, that of a privileged group capable of overthrowing social conventions. Visionaries with a new perspective on the world. Not bad as an idea, but I believe locking up and hitting the street to champion activism would mean masking a lot of my own internal weaknesses, which isn't my thing at all. "Why should I have sex when playing videogames for hours on end doesn't require half the effort?" asked one user on asexuality.org, AVEN's page, which is the line I try to avoid, though later on that same page there are also more self-parodying pieces such as a very witty one entitled "guide for asexuals in a sexual world."

Gays have their bears, their daddies, their tarts and their Adonises, amongst asexuals a kind of A-Pride is emerging – with its own palette of who you can be within it, from "aromantics" (who want to have nothing to do with the life of emotions either), to those who marry, and those who distinguish sex and love. Professor Bogaert again: "Asexuality will one day be more acceptable, but it will never be as powerful as the gay movement for one simple reason: fewer members. I hope that it will become a significant movement, that they join together, share information and feel close to one another." But I have my doubts, given that the "they can do what they like, as long as they do it behind closed doors" attitude to homosexuality has always seemed so wrong to me, there's no option but to put action ahead of intimacy, given that asexuality is socially invisible. This itself undermines the movement, but doesn't mean the efforts of raising awareness can be given up.

After this very odd Valentine's Day, it goes without saying that I was keen to carry out further research myself to try and find out what part of myself might be on this wavelength. Asexuality turned out to be an exceedingly flexible concept: there's something in it for everyone, which is in a way misleading, as well as running the risk that the concept might be accepted overquickly, almost, unbelievable as it seems, because it makes things easier. Eradicate sex because it creates conflict, it unbalances things. Going deeper and deeper, the fork in the path appeared before me: one way meant "taking sides", the other meant impartially recounting everything as it appeared before me, whether or not I felt part of it. Journalism, my vocation and an important part of my life, leaves honey on your lips from tasting a little of sundry subjects, which is good to stop you from overeating but not to make you of any use, least of all to yourself. This was asking a book of me. Essay, novel... I'd have to see what came. I started studying, I dived into chatrooms. Fascinating. Professor Bogaert sent me his reports. On Asexuality.org, as already stated, I came across new models for couples in which one the not-asexual member sought other "sexed" people. To me, this seems like an ideal option, though I'm all too aware of the difficulty of making it work. Such variety made me feel unable to commit to seeking a common cause and I found myself again feeling skeptical about the mass over the individual. And, when all's said and done, the "amoeba lifestyle" t-shirts made me laugh a lot. A lot a lot.

Since at the time I was doing a Philosophy MA (which I never finished), seeking a rigorous, specific perspective I turned to Foucault's History of Sexuality and away from Professor Bogaert, given that, according to Foucault, to enter into scientific terminology can be highly detrimental seeing that the "medicalization" of sex has been more detrimental to the individual and more useful to the control exerted by whichever Catholic power over the bedroom. This wide-ranging classification in which everything, though relatively permitted, has a label is, according to Foucault, the most counterproductive thing there is, an idea I'm pretty strongly in agreement with. And, opening myself up to the possibility of giving my book a more personal perspective, I spoken with my friend Fran, who I met, in fact, online and who has completed various university theses and has numerous scholarly articles to his name. When I was about to begun writing, he said that an "illustrated autobiography" might be the most honest path. "Narcissism can be tremendously fruitful," he said. "Look at Madonna." Say no more, I said!

Being serious now, clearly the considerable difference between this closet#1 and closet#2 is not the place of either historically, but the different kind of fear each generates, and how this then creates distinct minorities. As a homosexual, at least when I was first coming out to my friends and family, the risk you think you run with this revelation is social stigma, the possibility others will condemn you. Even to this day, like it or not, public confessions come with this underlying fear of rejection, fear of all that visibility brings with it, to greater or lesser degrees. But the risk an asexual runs when opening his or her heart (or however you want to put it) to the world is quite different: because asexuality is even less well known, he or she will get, but even more vehemently, the same as gays get: "it's just a phase, you'll get over it" (I remember how sad Clara looked saying that I was renouncing something truly wonderful), but the worst thing is thinking that this new condition, aspect or whatever you call it might ruin not so much the life of playing to the gallery but, lastly and when it comes down to it most importantly, the most private bastions of existence. Roughly, you can't help thinking that, unless you pass the sex exam, you'll never be accepted in the faculty of stable couples your whole damned life.

What Professor Bogaert disclosed to me wasn't all that timely, but it still seems to me that the freest and most honest thing to do is to speak for myself and myself only. I believe that there is something real, important and of substance in all this, but that doesn't mean I feel I can universalize my own experience. Nonetheless, surely when someone feels something, no one can claim it isn't authentic, even if it's arisen out of autosuggestion. It isn't the idea of laying myself bare that interests me so much as exposing and bringing understanding to a situation I consider complex, fluctuating, disconcerting. Eulogy and drama – not my thing. I merely want to understand and help others to understand. And then I remember something I heard from a sexologist I studied under and who struck me as a visionary in the field. When I was going round and round on the question of my sexual orientation, he talked about there being infinite intersexual states, and argued for a declassification of sexuality along the lines of Foucault's argument. "Here we are not talking about a diagnostic label," the sexologist once wrote to me, "but a biographical concept: in other words, diagnoses, in a surreptitious way, put aside the person, at least in the long term; but when biographical details are brought into the equation too (the things we tell to make sense of our lives), what we do then is include the person. And attraction, love-making, have different parameters nowadays, and women are no longer looking for the same things in a partner, and neither are men. The inter-sexual states, androgyny... they're on the map now." I myself would add, with his blessing and as a simplification, that asexuality is as well. And the face is, writing about oneself is also makes it harder for anyone to disagree with you, than if you say you're speaking for a whole group. So, anyway, to assume the disadvantages of honesty: to open up fully, without shame, avoiding the scholarly at all times and even at the risk that it will only end up as something persona-lly useful to me, I will try to overthrow this taboo with its highly unprovocative origins that are so provocative to me. Can you cause a scandal through a lack of sex? Yes, ironically. Can there by such a thing as a libertine without a sexual appetite? Let's see how we go.

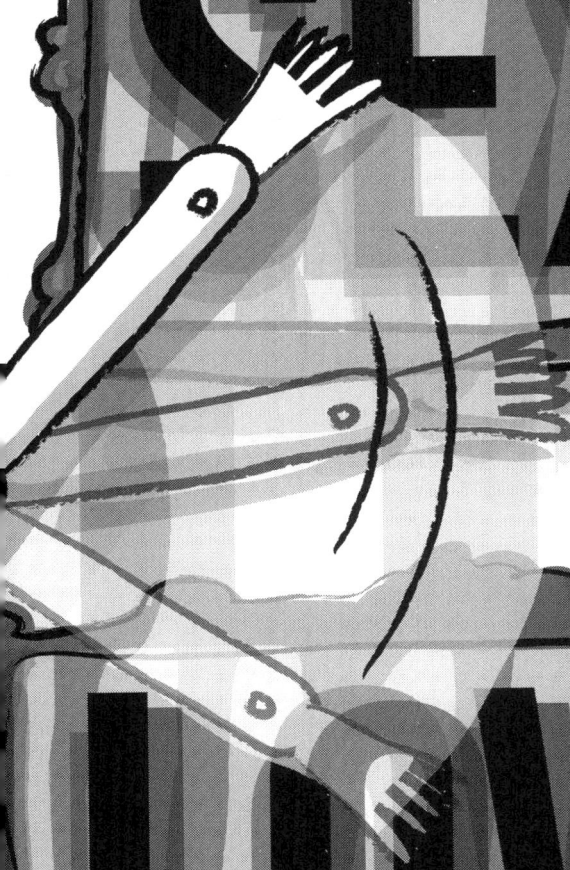

# SEX ORPHAN

I suppose it's nothing original or surprising for an absence to mark a life. Some people create a kind of spinal column for their existence out of rootlessness, out of seeking and never finding their place in the world. Others concern themselves with the lack of a maternal or paternal figure, a benchmark or a source of kindness during infancy. These are things people might or might not have, but for which substitutes can't be found, for all the talk about everyone being able to take the reins in their own life. Again, Madonna's an example, she's forever saying things like, sometimes she felt fulfilled, sometimes it didn't matter that her mother had died. But then she'd realize that wasn't the case and that, however she played it, she would always be an orphan. Along the way, some of her best songs she wrote were on the very subject. Girlfriend made the most of the hand she was dealt!

I'm lucky enough to have wonderful parents, but on the other hand I do feel myself to be something of a sexual orphan. Sex has been a phantasmal but ever present factor in my life's journey. In the same way that Marlon Brando didn't appear until the end of Apocalypse Now but was, through force of personality, still its protagonist – or, even more so, like the way Joan Fontaine in Rebecca was eclipsed by Maxime de Winter's late wife whose charisma was still everywhere. Nothing has more effect than what's not shown, right? In the same way that religious beliefs, which

I feel totally distanced from, awoke considerable though purely academic interest in me, sex is for me a kind of occult science exerting a strange and paradoxical power of fascination over me from without. Why wasn't I touched by sex's magic wand? It's a question I'll be asking till the day I die... or at least until for a fair few years yet. It's a childish feeling like "Ooh! I want one too!" that makes me feel like in the book Olvidado Rey Gudú (Forgotten King Gudú) by Ana María Matute in which the astonishingly noble and courageous mother Ardid, moved by spite and overweening, makes a pact in the hope that her son will never be touched by love. Has my story also got a touch of medieval fable about it? Mama, what did you do?

And just as there are some who go back to their first love, to the train they didn't catch, or start chopping onions every time they're sad and have no idea where their need to cry comes from, I always return to the existential slump produced by my sexual exclusion. In the rare moments that I do feel sorry for myself, it's always to do with my unsex.

As is the case with many things in life, when it comes to sex, effort doesn't cut it; sheer effort won't get you where passion, or genius, would. Milos Forman said the same thing in Amadeus. Talent alights by chance. In order to stand out, mediocrity must take refuge in determination, and in the moments when genius blunders, and also to show that in reality, working at something daily is the only reliable thing and the thing to be proud of. In my life I have had three great but not amorous passions: cinema, food and people. I've been variously successful in relation to each of these, but the affinities I've shown for them I had to work to cultivate. It's the least fair part of success in life: an already unlevel playing field that sometimes even disqualifies the talentless. I suppose this is why the Evangelist placates the least brilliant saying that God will judge us only according to the gifts we were given. I, for example, might have been given talents that might have made me more money... but I'm not complaining. And I haven't shown genius enough to put my case anywhere near that of Mozart vs Salieri. But the question is rather to do with how impotent someone can be in the very thing they weren't chosen to do; as much as they try, the passion just isn't in them, and they have to get there by way of effort. Then someone comes along who overtakes you with ease.

One day I realized I didn't have sex on the brain; it wasn't one of my innate gifts. I was eight years old and it all began when my older brother told a joke that made my mother and my six-year-old sister laugh. Our youngest sister (there are four of us) wasn't speaking by this point. I don't remember the joke that well, but it was something to do with some monks who mistook a man with a hard on for a slot machine and duly began rubbing his "stick" to the point semen came out, and them thinking it was moisturizer... Pretty awful really. And the thing was that my mother, who never avoided the subject of sex with us and, what's more, had bought each of us an Encyclopaedia of Sexuality for each of our respective ages, looked at me as though to say: where have you been all this time? A mother expects you not to pay attention when she tells you to squeeze the toothpaste from bottom to top, but hardly to zone out when she's explaining sex. Well then, she had to explain everything to me, right there at the table: the penis goes in the vagina (demonstrating with napkin rings, I remember it perfectly), the semen carries the "seed" etc... She might as well have been speaking Mandarin. Here she was, giving me the key to the thing everyone always talked about and that I never understood, but nonetheless I didn't have the feeling of not understanding. It was just passing me by, without me noticing it passing me by. So that was when I began to see that I was moving in a different orbit and that, in effect, I'd never paid attention to anything to do with sex. In spite of being a Madonna superfan by then! If the assumption is that the secret of her success is based on her eroticism...

Education in the Sancho Cardiel household was fairly sui generis. Like my mother and father, really. Both of them practicing Catholics, at that time in any case, but relatively conservatism. My father, due to his upbringing, is quite closed, but his sense of humor has always outweighed any blinkered attitude, which has meant he's always managed to maintain a sense of the values on which Christianit was founded (and has progressively forgotten). The feeling of respect and openness to the possibility that someone else might be right. Favoring conversation, understanding and very human, yes.

My mother's one of those who understands life and religion in a totally freestyle way, which is not to say arbitrarily. She'd never hesitate to point out, like Klaus Kinski, that Jesus also cracked the whip in the temple. A fascinatingly complex woman (I know this sounds like an uber-gay topic, but there you go), a pure improviser and someone who, though we all love our father very much, luckily took charge of our education while he was out earning the money. A super conventional setup, then, but miraculously avoiding all kinds of conventionalism. That's the key to my parents. And so when my mother defined sex she defined it as "a gift from God to compensate for all the pain in this life." When he heard that, little Mateo didn't turn it over much more in his mind.

I was very inquisitive, always asking questions. But never about sex. As a teacher in my highschool put it: "It worries me you don't have any doubts going into this exam. I don't have any doubts when it comes to the Basque language because I have zero idea how it's spoken." Something roughly similar might be applied to the state I was in – but seeing that my sister, two years younger than me, did understand the joke, and seeing my mother's surprise, I felt stupid – and I knew I wasn't stupid, because if there was one thing I'd heard all through my childhood it wasn't what a looker, or what a cutey, or what a joker, but how sharp this kid was. I shouldn't say it of myself, but there we are. Illustrated narcissism, did we say?

But anyway. Lots of children remain unaware of sex until puberty, it wasn't anything especially worrying that I was a little off the pace in that regard given everything else I had going for me. Puberty, however, was just around the corner and the gloves were off. Twelve years old. Winter's night. Nocturnal hardon. Flannel pyjamas. What's this sensation I feel if I frot my gland against the pyjamas? Huh? Huh? Huh, huh, huh, huh, huh... oops. What's this? I didn't mistake it for moisturizer, but it seemed I hadn't understood it in the joke either. And once more, sex and I had crossed paths by chance.

Now for the first clarification: asexuality and masturbation? Really, this was the first point of conflict in my possible identification with the new minority front. The answer to the question do I masturbate regularly is yes. But, though it sounds strange, in reality this has nothing to do with anything. The point is what moves the sexuality inside me. A well- meaning wank is a vent, a physiological necessity which, all in all, I consider to be less important than everything else. During my onanistic early years, my mind was a blank. A state that I alone achieved, no yoga, no nothing. Then men began to enter timidly into this excited imaginary.

My asexuality, in practice, is a far milder conflict than all this. In fact I sometimes think it's mostly a conflict just because it's difficult to categorize and the disorientation that goes with this difficulty – than because of anything inherently controversial about it. Because I can have sexual relations without going into "consensual violation". I experience it, at a given moment, like a medical consultation. There are certain parts of us that no one likes being rummaged around in, but if it has to be done, it has to be done, and I consider it neither an act of aggression nor do I emerge from a "consultation" feeling especially violated. Certain therapies, like physiotherapy, can even leave you feeling better. But not staggered. And not traumatized. So I've continued a practice for a number of years that really isn't the nicest thing, but I've ended up terming "sex out of courtesy". It could turn out to be more complicated to explain the whole thing than my usual approach – let him have what he wants (especially if he's put in the legwork) and drop my pants, or flee. Yes, I know, it's important to be assertive. But I usually resort to a recipe based on zooming out – abstracting mentally or spiritually from the situation – with a dash of curiosity to see what lies beneath these clothes (there's always something to be learned), plus a pinch of how much fun it is to relate the story with friends later on, topped off by the idea that I might even be pleasantly surprised and enjoy the thing. And it goes without saying that the failure to get it up has been a classic in my repertoire: being so cerebral about sex naturally means I'm more likely to get distracted. Which I've ended up calling "sex for the hell of it". But I've incorporated it so naturally into the process that it's even been funny to see the admiration you arouse in your sexual partner, man to man, when he realizes the low esteem in which you hold something that so many make such a song and dance about.

Certainly if I haven't, for whatever reason, satisfied my needs for any length of time, it shows in my body in the form of aggression or restlessness, but rarely in the form of desire. I function like an animal: I have the sexual impulse but I'm erotic-illiterate.

Somehow, masturbation turns into something else that has nothing to do with the structures that go with having a sexual relationship with another person. Like astronaut food for people who don't like sex. The body gets just what it needs, because the body goes on needing it. But in any case it avoids the bitter cup of having to face something three times a day that you take to be merely procedural. The quicker, the more clinical, the better.

Though sexuality is supposedly such an intimate thing, it still gets plastered all over public life. To the extent that, during many perfectly everyday conversations, when simply enjoying a walk through the city or going to watch a movie, I can't help but be reminded of the hurricane devouring cities and, life being what it is, I've been reserved the best seats in the eye of the storm, where all is calm and clear. As a homosexual I was never bothered by the offhand homophobia encoded in everyday phrases (there's a lot of reference to things like taking it up the ass in Spanish expressions), I've had more of a problem with things like "what you need is a good fuck" and the phrase we have in Spain for such people, which is "malafollá" and means someone who's bitter, uptight, frustrated – angry if they don't get their own way. I understand perfectly well the idea that turns of phrase don't mask malice but rather a less civilized earlier form of language, and that this is also one of our country's most refreshing characteristics. This being the case, I can't but avoid the thought: do I need a good fuck? Why am I not a bitter person though I never get a good fuck? I suppose it's just that the "malafollá" wants to and can't, and that's why they're frustrated. The result being, if I really don't want to, aside from the fact I'd like to be like everyone else, bitterness won't be generated. But I ask myself: why don't I want to if I really am able?

Professor Bogaert said to me in the interview, although it didn't make it into the article, that he was convinced that there was a biological element to asexuality. Maybe it's scientifically possible for the body of an asexual to neutralize the sexual impulse – the hormones, the prolacticine and the like – so I decided to have myself tested, thinking that, since I don't suffer the usual torments of a "malafollá", the most logical explanation must be physical. But the results were all in order – so could it be that the body itself is capable of neutralizing the hormones etc? If the mind is able to block out hunger, tiredness or even menstruation, why wouldn't the body be able – on its own account, quite apart from anything psychological – to neutralize the libido? From what I know, antidepressants have that effect. And being someone for whom that's normal, that personally I find it difficult to see my lack of desire as a defect. This is how I've been my whole life and I consider myself a fairly well-balanced person. Obviously, that isn't really for me to say… and the things that have arisen in the writing of this book have begun to make me doubt it, actually.

But then another important question. With adolescence comes not only sexual awakening, but also the more or less definitive formation of the identity. Now, looking back, I wonder about the extent to which my identity assembled around this lack of desire. As happens with a lot of homosexuals, who unconsciously postpone their sexual awakening and become model teenagers – just to upbraid what's supposed to be happening them, ie. hormonal revolution, ie. irascibility – only later to break out, asexuality can turn the transition to adulthood into a relatively calm experience. When I came out to my father he said, not straight away but at some point soon after, something along the lines of "I was too good to be true". And though I've never been gruff or unsociable in character I think that, due to other things, it's true that to take the sexual impulse out of adolescence would alleviate a lot of the difficulties associated with presenting oneself in society.

Clearly, revenge is a dish best served cold, and there are some steps that can't be skipped. My parents, after reading this book, would say they would much rather I had been a feverish, impossible teenager than having to see such raw material written down for all the world to see.

Sometimes I look again at my sixteen year old self and I think I was a little unforgiving of certain people who, really, were doing what they had to do by law – which is what comes of being a teenager who was climbing up the walls. When a few years go by and the symptoms don't subside, the general opinion is that it's unusual, but at that age it's totally the norm. At the time, for me it came through as very similar to a lack of selfcontrol, becoming an animal in the face of a rationality that I thought defined and gave prestige to all human beings. I didn't feel different: I felt calmer. More mature, if you like. A little superior, I might as well admit it. But now, with hindsight, I think how absurd it was to tell a fifteen year old off for being immature. And my supposed maturity in fact obscured a deep ignorance of what goes with being human through life's various stages. What I'm saying is that I was the most immature out of everyone – even though the adult world will love hearing that.

I was also laboring under a self-imposed yoke that it has taken me many years to liberate myself from. I remember feeling ashamed for making a spelling mistake when I was six years old or for having spilt something on an old man's clothes at a birthday party when I was seven. In what I thought of as my role, I wasn't supposed to cause problems. And sometimes I've got to the point of wondering if something inside me inhibits sex by considering it a problem in itself.

I also remember, at university in Madrid, arguing with some friends I was sharing a dorm with because they weren't taking responsibility for their bad marks in June having had a whale of a time their whole final year, especially those of them less disposed to study. And what did they expect? I was the one asking. What should I expect of myself? Someone should have answered me.

This has always been the burden that's weighed on me: I've fought to build a coherent identity, because for me it was something relatively easy and I saw that it would win me the approval of others. But it escaped me that, clearly, there's something I don't feel but that is exactly the thing people do to familiarize themselves with not always being in control, and in living with it a large part of personal growth also resides.

For all that, inevitably, a part of me was being left behind, not moving beyond puerile in this specific regard. In the end, trying to fill the void of sex in me has also left me such a long way out of bounds that I've become familiar with the uncontrollable parts of myself and this, ultimately, has made me more complete. I have been getting closer to this reality and realizing that, over and above this no-loose-end behavior of mine, for a number of years a greater contradiction has appeared than that which I see day to day in others.

My identity formed without the influence of blind impulses and, added to the fact that in general I kept to – I keep to – Christian values of respect and goodness, egoism turned out to be something that was relatively easy for me to eradicate. But contrary to what most people believe, this isn't in fact a good thing. I believe that the struggle against egoism begins in the certainty that the ego cannot be eradicated, because it is inside of us. That is why it has to be controlled and kept on the safe side, so it doesn't get out of hand. Nonetheless, without being the most impulsive person, it was unusual for me to ever say anything inappropriate and for years I was able, not to crush altogether, but yes to suppress the individualist impulse – very effectively. I was a faithful, reliable support. A still lake. While my brother went off the rails smoking weed and my sister was getting into mohicans, I was very careful about staying balanced. I concerned myself with others of man's restless qualities. Years later, I would come to reject culture as something that could possibly carry sophisticated emotions, though in its moment it was something my family and friends enjoyed. They also thought how mature I was. I channeled my restlessness doing radio shows and writing for the newspaper, developing a savage capacity for memorizing everything to do with cinema (not only the Oscars) and, like an aperitif to what it would later become, feeling a powerful attraction for abstract emotions. Out of that grew a number of courtly loves, in the old style, with certain female 'muses' that I encountered at high school. I still have a number of love letters that continue to move me because they are truly pure and, therefore and in spite of everything, also beautiful. Thanks to that, I haven't disconnected from the world entirely, because identity, humility and passion are also germinated in love.

I must have seemed quite a character. A rare bird for whoever wanted to appreciate it and a laughing stock in high school. But on the inside I had an unshakeable resolve – partly because at home I felt as highly valued as could be – that everyone else had it wrong, so much so that I couldn't care less what – if I'm honest this is the only way I can put it – a battalion of bumpkins thought of me.

In effect, in good humor and with constantly decent manners, I was turning into the worst kind of snob. My life was in danger of going into autopilot: my day s during the last year at high school reduced to the six hours of class, one hour of dinner, another for siesta, three on the internet or watching a Madonna concert – always the same one, the Blond Ambition Tour – dinner and bed. The three central elements experienced from the sofa. Clear indicators of depression, but the fact was I wasn't sad. I was relatively happy, in my way. Going to dance class a couple of times a week gave me the feeling of being active. Looking at it now, save for the conversations I had with my family, the laughs we shared at the dinner table, and the one or two friends I had, living like that seems totally awful to me. And after being in Madrid, every time I went back to the countryside for anything more than three weeks I asked myself how I could have put up with it for more than ten years without throwing myself off the balcony. I'd get so anxious that I'd end up unwell, even having dandruff attacks. How lovely.

Luckily, and even though I hate this kind of reasoning, coming out was a great opportunity for me. Not because being gay is the greatest thing in the world these days, but because, in my case, it allowed me to rectify these unyielding tendencies, those that were troubling to me as well as those that other people found troubling. Mateo had suddenly had a huge internal shift, smiling all along, and there he was, faultless and even happy. My parents worked it out pretty quickly: it was too good to be true, something had to be up. Maybe I had a lot to deal with. I realized along the way that if I wasn't there to act as a support, it would be ok. I'd been overestimating my role as stabilizer in the family nucleus. It meant I could also be a focus for conflict and ask for support because my family, luckily, also knew how to give me that, to step up when things were tough and offer alternative and calming perspectives. Which they did, once they'd overcome the shock; I still remember my poor mother as she was coming to terms with the situation, with tears in her eyes, coming up with a delirious off-the-cuff theory about her tolerance for homosexuals being due to a passion for Greek philosophy. "There, they all were," was her Parthian shot, which took to be affectionate in spite of the situation's emotional charge.

In any case, if there are things that are done late in life and badly, this wasn't one of those cases. I don't believe the cost was that great, but at 18 years of age I was at a time of reorienting my character. And though the way was paved for me to turn into a misfit, one of life's rejects, it all went fairly gradually and, yes, reasonably. Suddenly there was margin for error in my life. Especially in my peculiar relationship with sex, this great event by which pride, virility and power are measured, and which therefore took me down a peg or two, or maybe a few more than that. Being so promising in so many of the things I'd turned my hand to, so faultless, I won't deny that it was a surprise to turn to sex and find myself such a hopeless case. Not in terms of output (all normal on that front), but in terms of enjoyment. It isn't that I experienced it as a defeat, because it wasn't something that my body aspired to achieve. Nor was it that its absence was reflected in frustration. But it made me readjust, once again, the rubric for such important things in life as satisfaction, pleasure seeking and personal development. I became familiar, in short, with what it is to have limitations and sympathized with feeling hung-up, which, curiously enough, is actually a positive thing for someone who tends to be a perfectionist.

Separating the wheat from the chaff resulted in a combination with which, nowadays, I'm fairly satisfied. Which is to say: I haven't given up my dedication to the people in my life who have brought me great, great happiness, but the thing is that excess has also entered into my various behaviors. I've flirted with disaster from time to time, but the waters have always ended up flowing back to their source. And now I've turned into a truly unfocused person, but more fun at the same time. I suppose I've become more human, but something of the angel is still in me. And no one can take away the good times I've had. Years on and in my professional life I'm still relying on all the knowledge I accumulated when I was a teenager. And this has put me at a certain advantage, which in turn has led me to have a relatively successful career; I'm even in a position to take the afternoon off every now and then. Better than nothing.

But this 'orphanhood', which though I continue to accepting it, still affects and hurts me, and may need toning down. It isn't a fullblown orphanhood, but something closer to a childhood spent in a hospice, where one never gives up hope that adoptive parents might show up one day. That sex might arise, epiphanylike. To quote Georges Bataille's Eroticism, which has been fundamental to me in the writing of this book: "Erotic experience linked with reality waits upon chance, upon a particular person and favorable circumstances". So that later they say that I'm very lucky. Twenty-eight years old and still waiting.

# INSCRUTABLE ARE THE PATHS OF ATTRACTION

It would make sense, putting aside an interest in sex, to think that the asexual lives in a somehow more objective reality, one in which friendship comes uppermost in personal relations. Nope! One more myth to knock down. In fact I consider myself to be someone with a large seductive impulse and I feel attracted to people all the time. Attraction isn't emotional, it's physical, even if it doesn't feed into something sexual. At first sight, I've often felt attracted to people, but just as often not – and the look on my friends' faces is then often "what are you thinking, Mateo?". So as not to get carried away by sex's illogic, you might be a little less scattershot, aim for the usual kinds of beauty, for example...

But at what point can sex be considered to have its beginnings? Maybe instead of talking in terms of "asexuality" we should say "a-relation-sexual", because that's when, precoitus (or pre-whatever), the difference begins. If this weren't the case and, given how much more socially acceptable it is to have relationships with people of the opposite sex, why complicate my life by feeling physically attracted to men? If my true vocation is really to stay at home and look after my children... how ironic! In theory, the only advantage is the fact that there are many people who, wrongly, think that asexuality is the preamble to homosexuality, so I hope that the approaching the question from the opposite direction might strengthen the idea that asexuality isn't necessarily only about same-sex attraction.

The mantra "I don't focus on the body, I'm interested in someone's mind" ought, almost by definition, to make bisexuals of asexuals. But in fact it's nothing like that. Because, I do read bodies, and these bodies have neither vaginas nor breasts. And I hear masculine voices that attract me. I've seen men who it's quickened my heartrate just to look at them, without saying a single word. It isn't a question of sensitivity to beauty, because I also see beauty in women. I've wanted to kiss them, I've wanted to touch and embrace them, I've wanted to take their clothes off and have in fact done so when I've had the chance; but my satisfaction threshold doesn't require anything after that. In some way or other I assume, and I repeat, getting involved like this doesn't feel violent or tiring, that once this point is reached it requires a lot of confidence and a lot of assertiveness to say "this is where we've got to" because very often at this point the thing that comes into my head is "you're not asexual, what you are is a prick tease." Any external perspective is suddenly shut off to me. It might sound surreal, but my upbringing and my good manners win out – I can't be rude! But what's for definite is that my impulse to initiate the seduction ritual comes to me with a naturalness that doesn't carry through into a desire for penetration, masturbation or fellatio. Neither giving nor taking. How can this be? The fact is, it just is. And my degree of satisfaction leaving just before the party starts is stupendous. I head home feeling fit to burst.

In any case, the seduction process continues to be one of my life's great pleasures. I love flirting and, although it often clashes with my not very sexed nature, I've learned not to repress this part of myself, and to simply face the consequences and deal with the usual predetermined outcome. I've never had anyone force me when I've said "enough". But then again I haven't always said it.

Travel is something else I love and, at the risk of sounding frivolous, I must admit that part of what I enjoy is people watching – Paris, New York, Italian people mainly – though it's quite another thing to catch people's eyes – Berlin and Oslo I heart you, Rome and Paris I hate you. It's intriguing the way that, according to local taste, a person can go from being any old face in the crowd to exotic and attractive. They say are no ugly people, only less full cups. But by the same token, almost everyone could find a longitude and latitude at which their beauty will be beheld.

In any case, I have fonder memories of a visit if on one of its nights a man should happen to fall into my arms. That's all I need. A couple of good kisses do the trick. And since I'm single and travel with work, I've made every trip and every assignment profitable, be as it may with this kind of infinite stretching out of adolescent relations.

These frontiers between what is sexual and what's not create a lot of confusion in me. A confusion not solely to do with not giving my "partenaire" a release, but, although prompted by sexual relations, something that I've found functions differently in me. The chemistry I sometimes feel with someone in the street, or in conversation, or in a club, has decided to make itself quite independent of the chemistry I feel later on in bed. Might a new way of considering the breakdown between physical and purely sexual be put forward? From what I see around me, people know full well whether someone excites them sexually – even with clothes on – based on their demeanor. Since I'm somewhat illiterate sexually, it isn't until we're getting down to it that I'm able to draw any conclusions. I don't know what I like in bed and until I don't taste it I can't tell, which, as you might imagine, turns every sexual encounter into uncertainty, into a national lottery. How can taste be refined in this sense? For my own good and that of other people, it would be good to come up with a formula. I don't know what's worse: having chemistry with someone only to end up making a shopping list in your mind as he's trying to conclude what, in many cases, you initiated, or giving it a go with someone who you wouldn't have thought worth it and then being pleasantly surprised. Ideally, obviously, the physical and the sexual coincide. If not, there's a lot of arduous explaining to do, too arduous for a fling that, most likely, will occur under the influence. (You can always blame the lack of a hardon on the alcohol).

But although it would be make sense for this confusion to make me selective and prudent, unfortunately the reverse is true. Everyone's self-confidence is built in part on feedback from others, and the mirror we find in wooing is one of the most important. Being attractive is comforting, just as the opposite creates insecurity. So I come back from Rome, a society clothed in chaos but in the final analysis highly predictable and full of archetypes, with a tremendous sense of rejection because there was space – or I didn't find one – for flirting. Is this ego-need greater than the non-need for sex? Maybe this is another answer to the theory that this lack of appetite arises out of sexual stage fright. In fact, increasingly, my sexual encounters are becoming placid rather than abrupt or in any way rough. A strange placidity generated, I'd say, because my self-acceptance is coming along slowly.

I recently went to bed with a guy whom I'd met again for the first time in years. He said I was much more relaxed – and I didn't know if that was a good or a bad thing. Sex didn't use to drive me; it obstructed me. Now not even that. Yes, when it comes to being in a relationship, I'm still a long way from achieving placidity. Sex definitely isn't something that has caused any of the breakups I've been through, even if my longest relationship was only a year and a half and, when all's said and done, it's fair to say that in that case I self-imposed (not in a Calvary way) a sexual frequency at about the level of what "society expects". But it's all a juggling act, and everyone is always trying to work out "the real reasons" behind this "sex just isn't my bag" attitude. They try to help you solve it, but only fuel it, generate more anxiety. The impotence of seeing, on the one hand, that you'll never be at the level your partner demands; the muddle you get in if you're on the receiving end of such a lot of patience, so much understanding – directed at a part of you that you really feel is part of you and that won't change for all the concerned attention in the world; and the sensation that it creates a rift in a relationship with someone marvelous, given how difficult it is to even get to this point. Add it all together and you've got a pretty substantial mess. And I say again that sex itself never ends up being the cause of a breakup, but I always have a nagging doubt as to its tangling influence, or if, really, it is the seed for the tensions. The phantasm of "is this the person who's going to fulfill me in the long term" raises its head so easily (a silly way to approach things, for sure), but the pea under the mattress of the relationship – the fear that you'll never have a "straight-forward" sexual life – becomes a huge obstacle even if you find someone who empathizes with your asexuality.

Ideally in these cases you'd find someone with the same appetites as you. That is: who only wants it every so often. But let's crunch the numbers: if we say that 50% of people are men and 50% women, and 20% of these are homosexual, we're talking about a 10%. Further, if we say that between 1 and 5% of the population is asexual, we're saying that, in the best case scenario, 0.5% of the population are my "target". Out of them, have a go at finding one who you like physically, is a good conversationalist, likes you and is at a point of wanting a relationship. Mission impossible, basically. And we have to bear in mind that, in this case, not having sexual desire doesn't prevent you from attracting those who do. Given that for homosexuals the transgression of seducing a heterosexual is always exciting, but the almost total impossibility of success means that one ends up accepting the glaring facts: whether or not we're peas, we're bound to end up in the same pod. Whereas the lack of sexual desire is a bomb that needn't be revealed til the end – that's if you want to drop it at all. What a mess.

There are very different solutions to this conflict. The easiest is to carry your cross alone: satisfy your partner's desires and at points take the initiative yourself, understanding it to be a "sacrifice" to prevent the relationship from deteriorating, which is the ultimate aim of everyone who goes along with this. But the emotional wear and tear is sometimes just too high. And on paper it obviously sounds somewhat humiliating, for all that it might end up becoming a routine. On the other hand, even if you're able to maintain sexual relations that are, let's say, conventional, or you managed to be relatively creative with it, for all that it might be very pleasurable, the thought is always there: get it over with.

A kind of "obligation" hangs over the act of sex, and I've never been able to undo the wish for a quick orgasm. The consequence being that, for someone like me, the nightmare word has a synonym, and that synonym is Tantra.

The solution – perfect in theory but very tricky in practice – is the acceptance of the requirements: to make your partner understand your disinterest in sex or your very infrequent need for it without them taking it personally, without their self-esteem taking a hit. And so we come to one of my favorite concepts: division. Bearing in mind that a relationship between a couple is nourishing in many ways, expecting your every need be met is fanciful. Even my mother says it: "no-one's going to totally fulfill you". But it's just as naïve to think that a couple can function if the one who has a normal amount of sexual desire isn't satisfied. Or, more than naïve, it's ambitious: because it would mean shifting so very many conceptual poles – in the individual as well as in society... To add in a third person is an option, obviously, but that requires a lot of maturity and a lot of security in the amorous bond (and this takes time) to not fall into comparing oneself – in a "ménage a discord" – so that the third person appears to have everything one of the other two needs.

On the other hand, maturity is also needed on the part of the "sexed" member in the relationship, so they don't collapse in the face of being with someone that they can't arouse, for all they might be able to feel their love. It's strange, but an asexual can end up making the sexed partner feel sexually unsure of themselves; they have to understand, through thick and thin, this "it's nothing personal" thing. I have to admit that, facing this tired companion – not getting it up – it's been less reproaches than "what's up? I don't excite you?" that I've had to deal with. Asking for empathy in these cases is a bridge too far. And, of course, it can be that the member who does need sexual satisfaction doesn't understand sex if it isn't linked to love, or doesn't consider it to be the preferred form, and in this case the division I'm talking about can become a separation lacking the synergy that arises in the fusion of both disciplines. Am I hoping for a non-existent perfection?

This is why with the passing of time there comes a kind of light at the end of the tunnel for the asexual mentality. Luis Buñuel said in his autobiography My Last Sigh that he felt a certain relief when he reached old age and found that his sexual impulse decreased at the same time that his skin became wrinkled and his body became. The beast had been tamed. Whereas a lot of people claim that old age by no means excludes a sex life in the same way that neither does childhood and that man is an erogenous being from cradle and grave. I believe physical deterioration happens, indisputably, which means I've often felt prematurely old in terms of sexuality. Strangely, ever since I was young, autumn romances in cinema have held an atypical fascination for me. Robin and Marian , with its wonderful depiction of decrepit love, was the first movie that made me cry. And I felt that, once I was through the usual frisky years, the world would "come down to my level" when the sun set, and I would be a great lover in the autumn of my life.

One day we were driving with my mother and father and she – this is so like her – say to my father: "I'm a little worried because I'm not as interested in sex as before." My father answered: "My darling, we're in the same boat." And it's one of the most beautiful things I've witnessed in my entire life. Will old age therefore be my golden age? Overly ingenuous desires, I sense.

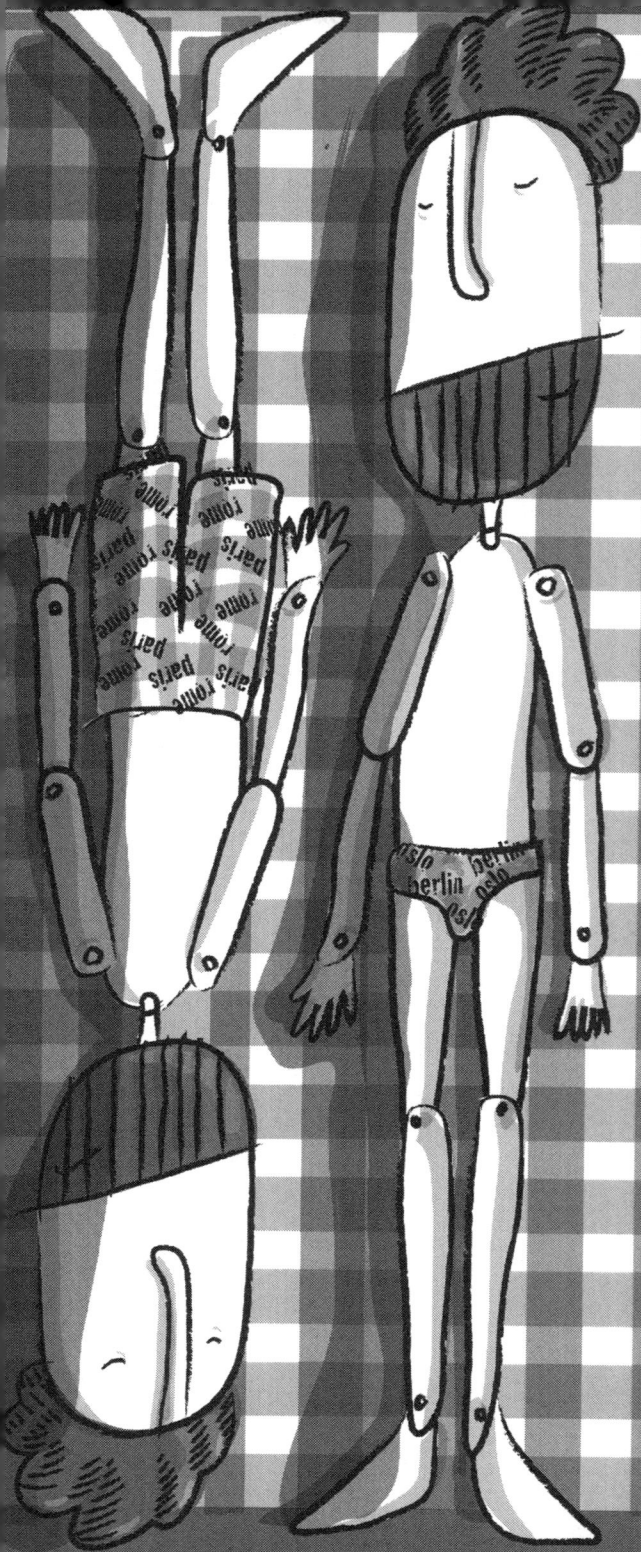

# LIGHT

# INTIMACY AND INNOCENCE

If before I talked about an identity marked by a lack of desire, a deeper analysis also makes me unsure as to how much this asexuality is the product of two concepts that have developed in me of their own accord and that are strongly linked with the erotic: intimacy and innocence. Produced what? Difficult to know exactly.

Since we journalists are so keen on definitions, I'll quote the definition for "intimate" according to the Real Academia de la Lengua. Leaving aside the anecdotal mention that in Cuba it can mean "sanitary towel", intimate means "the innermost, the most internal", and in reference to a friendship it means "very close" and to a friend "very dear and trusted". For me, sex tallies with none of these things.

My way of talking about sex so freely can be a little startling but it isn't actually to do with have been around the block (in fact I haven't gone anywhere) so much as the fact that sex reveals nothing of intimacy to my conscious self and therefore it isn't worth being discreet. My distanced experience of sexual relations – my attitude is somewhere between apathy, disdain, and simply seeing it as another triviality – turns them into the antithesis of the "strip away body and soul" thing it means for large numbers of people. I feel bad for the psychoanalysts and for Tennessee Williams (one of my favorite playwrights, nonetheless) but I'm just not like that. Maybe the social dictatorship of sex makes me want to be in the same line of submission to desire, or maybe I have a little bit of a problem with my difference in this regard, but that's as far as sex affects me. Orphanhood, that's what we've said it is.

With the idea of an intimate friend not only as someone close to you, but someone whose friendship with you someone else might draw conclusions about you through. Your friends are a reflection of you, for good or ill, but I don't feel as though sex is a prism through which I can be observed and deciphered. Though I'm still trying to work out why, sex clearly isn't my friend. And transparency with respect to my practices, my feelings, my opinions and sexual problems is absolute. I don't feel feeble talking about my minimal sexual output, just as I talk openly my other failings that might have negatively affected a friend or a family member. What's failing to get a hard compared with a betrayal?

When it comes to sex I don't find anything particularly embarrassing. And that could be the key to this disconnect with the erotic, given that, as Georges Bataille put it, eroticism arose "when man began moving imperceptibly from unashamed sexuality to sexuality with shame". In Spain, male genitals are very often referred to, I don't know if affectionately, as "las vergüenzas" – the naughties – and ever since I was young I've been perfectly prepared, not at all ashamed, to get my naughties out. I was something of an infant exhibitionist and there's still a bit of that in the adult me. Once I got through the period during which

I feared showing my genitals in a male locker room, and an unexpected reaction, might reveal my sexual orientation, now I'm back to being fairly immodest. I think it's from my family – in my house being naked was totally normal. In fact, I sometimes think I go through life in general naked – love, friendship, or even my work, in its creative aspect, I think is far more revealing than sex – and this means that even when I am literally naked, I hardly notice the difference. Maybe my overarching lack of sexual appetite has brought me not so much to rejection as a kind of naturalization of sexuality. And, now I come to it, something in me feels obliged – and I'm aware I'm not sure where this comes from – not to lie, not to hide essential details. I feel as though my female friends (and I could swear this isn't the case) expect to hear what I've been up to and, if I don't tell them all about it, I'm hiding something. To sum up, I think I'm a little but of a bigmouth when it comes to the subject of me.

How does this bring me, then, to terrain as private as sentimental relations? My indiscretion when it comes to talking about sexuality, of course, is less in evidence when I do feel respect for the person I'm involved with sexually. I'm not brainless, and like anyone, I do shut up from time to time. And for the same reason, in keeping with the utter honesty of this account, when it comes to it I'll also change the names and personal details of my lovers for the sake of their privacy. For a boyfriend or lover who has problems accepting their sexuality, embarking on a relationship with me can mean a rapid acceleration through the six degrees of separation – because of the expansiveness of my social circle, they'll effectively have come out within a week. But in terms of the sex, that experience remains between my partenaire and me. Because therein lies another coiled intimacy that I am prone to: that of love.

How, therefore, can my sexual relations be interpreted from a psychological or psychoanalytical point of view? Would they consider me repressed or frigid? I certainly tick some of the boxes: perfectionist, homosexual in a conservative milieu... Do I go on about it to compensate for my disconnection from the act itself? Verbosity may reflect incapacity. Does it actually show that my self-assuredness is actually a farce and I'm just too fucked up to fuck? Show me your assumptions and I'll show you everything you lack. My sexuality's thought of as having nothing to do with interaction? Bearing in mind that I do masturbate, maybe a phobia of shared sex should be considered. Radical narcissism? Well, I mean, I do try to offer the things I'd like to find in someone else, but... And on and on. I find psychoanalysis very thought-provoking, but there's always the booby trap of the fact that human beings are so complex that almost every single theory can be a fertile field, you could see very decent yields from any such ideas. But from that to being the crux of the matter, is quite a leap.

I can find causes or previous experiences that justify my relationship with sex, same as everything. But what if all of them were overinterpretations of a reality that's actually far more straightforward, a simple question of appetites? How this non-intimate relationship with sex has meant the explosion of social structures is a different thing altogether.

Intimacy also means closeness. And sex not only creates a distanced relationship between it and myself, but in some cases it's also served to push my sexual partners away. Not only because sometimes going to bed with someone on a first date is the best way to make sure they won't phone you again (they've got what they wanted out of you and vanish), but because I'm more old-fashioned: if I don't believe the context is right, if there's not enough common feeling, the sexual relation will take on too much prominence within the body of experiences between myself and said person. In the same way that people disguise pills for their pets so they eat them without realizing, I end up stretching the moment out until I'm convinced that – if, as usual, I don't enjoy the experience very much – it doesn't have too much specific weight within the relationship and doesn't remove entirely – my desire to see them again.

So what does intimacy consist of for me? A tendency for sincerity is actually one of my distinctive features, because if there is something I lack, as well as sexual appetite, that's secrets. When I was small my mother had to be very careful with what she told me because I'd blurt it out unchecked to a teacher at my elementary school, who ended up knowing all my family's gory details but never wrote a biography because we weren't famous. So I learned, more or less, to know what and what not to say to other people, so as not to disappoint. But self-censure still isn't my strong point. I'm still that guy, the one who doesn't know to hold back details just in case, or the other thing is that I'll actually forget things if I don't share them. On the one hand, this makes sense bearing in mind that I'm not generally a regretful person, and I'm not embarrassed by my mistakes. Those kinds of naughties I never cover up. My friend Toni, whom I met studying philosophy, with his usual cogency, said he thought I had a problem with intimacy as a concept, which really made me think. I think he hit the nail on the head. What is my intimacy? I mean: mine, just mine. Truth: it doesn't exist.

Why so forthcoming? Why do my secrets burn inside me? Clara told me that people who don't know me find it hard coming to understand that I'm always telling the truth. And my greatest truth is that I'm a terrible liar. I'm a terrible trickster, I'm awful at ambiguity. I find lying hard going – it even makes me panicky. I feel that lying discredits me as a person. It's another thing to sometimes be unclear, because I myself am unclear about something, but this complexity, visible from outside, really is what's within me.

What are the secrets in my head for? It's quite likely that there are even some secrets that remain hidden from me. But is sex incompatible with my usual transparency? What's innuendo – such an important factor in sensuality – if not concealment, theatricality, enticement? The function of secrets is not to betray people. As for me, I can't betray myself, which makes no sense make sense. But if you lie to yourself aren't you also betraying yourself?

Or am I betraying myself by not retaining a modicum of privacy? If secrets are a person's best parts, why not share them? And if they're the worst, why shut them up and let them turn musty? I know this reasoning is very naïve, but that's what goes through my head. A head that tends to communicate everything and that, as my mother said, needs a filter.

It might sounds foolish, but I have to conclude that my intimacy is actually something collective. Shared in a larger circle than is perhaps usual, and because of this, on the one hand, people naturally have the feeling of being close to me, because I let it escape into wider than usual spaces and, in these spaces, people appreciate being given special access. In turn, other people see a place in me to share things they've never shared with anyone.

So here's the rub, again: the thing that defines me and that I enjoy in people, also discredits and limits me sexually. As Nieves said, I don't experience it as a problem, but I can see how people who are more reserved distrust such openness. Because they assume that everyone holds about 20% back out of self-preservation, they themselves will therefore tend to add that 20% on – and take you even more seriously. No one, it seems, is so innocent as to not keep a few cards close to their chest.

And so we come to innocence, with which I have an ever more complicated relationship. Lots of films and books make a connection between sexual awakening and the loss of innocence. I don't know if I can say I never lost mine, because I'm by no means a naïve person, but from my at times absurd level of candor it seems determined not to say goodbye. And it broke out during an apparently normal incorporation into "active adult life" (as the social worker called it). And it connects me to this angelic spirit with which my mother summed up the whole question.

What mental strings are pulled by intimate sexual contact in order to eradicate innocence? "I could never again be an angel. Innocence, once lost, can never be regained," said Neil Gaiman. But "there's no aphrodisiac like innocence", as Jean Baudrillard said, and maybe this is the final secret of my success… I'm not sure. I suppose that in the end it's as simple as it is to pair sex with our entrance into the world and infancy with innocence – two suppositions that I consider erroneous. But, curiously, if there is something that's stayed constant in me since I was a child, and that I haven't managed to get rid of, it's the innocence that makes me susceptible to believing practically everything a person says, if I respect that person. This has led me to believe in the impossible. I'm a man of faith – though not in a religious sense.

As with all children, my most reliable source was my parents. And up to this very day I feel I'm being naughty if I watch TV with the lights off, if I drink water after eating fruit or go for a swim too soon after eating. In situations as normal as when your schoolmates tell you there's no such thing as Santa, it didn't even occur to me that my parents might could lie to me. They explained it to me later and I understood their reasons for doing it – they seemed legitimate to me. There was no letdown. Out of my four brothers, I was clearly the one who had least problems with our upbringing; I accepted pretty much all of their teaching precepts, for all that they were opposed to homosexuality and had a conservative view on certain things. But in essence, everything was very logical and they imparted some truly, unreservedly, decent sentiments. I didn't simply accept their authority, rather, I checked their criteria carefully. I never lied to them, because it seemed wrong, bearing in mind the trust they always placed in us. And I always told my brothers off when they abused that trust, or wanted to try out in the crafty teenager role. With the parents we had! But I did all this, clearly, ignorant of the fact that rebellion goes hand in hand with and individual's independent growth.

What I'm trying to get at is the feeling I have that made me believe so wholeheartedly what my mother said about sex being "a gift from God to make up for all the bad things in life" and how I came to understand that, in a life with more happiness in it than sadness, sex had no place, because this meant the compensatory action was no longer necessary. Is my problem simply that I take things too literally? Sometimes I think my relationship with sex can be characterized as, on the one hand, a letdown of gigantic proportions, and, on the other, blind belief. Disappointment would be prompted by a tendency to glorify something that, definitely, isn't all that. When I tell people around me that I don't enjoy sex and explain the whys, a lot of them empathize or make comments like "man, of course! Sex really isn't that great." I also see that there are some who have a relatively absent sex life and yet they're calm about it, without having to think about defining it as asexuality or whatever other nonsense. Was I hoping for too much from sex – do I in fact not have an unusual relationship with sex – am I just denying this simple truth? There's something of this in it, though it seems weak as a principle cause.

I'm not saying I'm the only one to speak simple truths, but when it comes to sex, it's hard to overemphasize people's tendency to tangle their discourse up in what's expected of them and, within "the Emperor's new clothes" syndrome, a tendency also for a complexity to arise that's both fairly unnecessary and harmful. The classic "I've got this friend who" line, bringing about a chain reaction of fuck after fuck after fuck, both stray into caricature, but how many people are there who in fact hide immense frustrations beneath an apparently totally successful sex life? I'm not trying to recruit people to my 'sect' but there is a point in this society where we really do find ourselves in a sex dictatorship – with all the classic touches: politics aimed at the greater glory of the Leader and the silencing of any opponents to the regime – we should at least acknowledge the mechanisms of sex a little better and thereby improve not so much our performance as our satisfaction.

Sex, again in terms of intimacy, reveals itself through half measures and, in general, is explained pretty badly. When I was at university, also under the auspices of seeking different sexualities, I did a project on the sexuality of people who are born blind. This gave me a chance to put two and two together – to add up the flawed, sentimental nature of sex education and the exaggerated effect of its application to someone who, as a blind person, has such difficulty filling in this part of the syllabus that most of us carry out in our own extra curricular explorations. How can you do that if you need someone to guide you the whole time?

The blind people were a kind of mirror for the opacity and half-truths usually contained in sex education, something that for obvious reasons was even worse a few decades ago, when blind adolescents didn't even receive clear explanations on anatomy. Presented with an orthopedic model of the female body, most of them thought the genitals were situated at the top of the sternum. Not to mention the fact that blind organizations totally disregard pornographic material or erotic literature – which could be useful resources were they turned into Braille.

Though this is an extreme case, and disregarding my own innocence or credulity for a moment, society does peddle a false or at least heavily simplified version of sex. To start with, it's poorly explained. Secondly, it's so centered on coitus. Throw in the fact it's male-oriented through and through, and finish off with its utter removal from reality. Distorted, in other words.

According to Foucault, this mirror play is altogether necessary. "The essential point is that sex was not only a matter of sensation and pleasure, of law and taboo, but also of truth and falsehood, that the truth of sex became something fundamental, useful, or dangerous, precious or formidable: in short, that sex was constituted as a problem of truth," and he, clearly, considered it an abomination to turn sex into some luminous, diaphanous space, free of secrets and with total, unqualified exposure. It's a different thing to reveal to the point of eradicating spontaneity, the feeling of discovery, than it is to lie deliberately and create false public images. For that, it's better to keep your peace. And that everyone, out of their own darkness, create their own rules to govern their own image and likeness.

In terms of honesty, women traditionally appear more inclined to accept their problems and open up about them, although in the past they weren't so intent on satisfaction and showed a more conformist attitude in that respect. But in men there's a great contradiction between how important they consider sex to be and how rarely they define, communicate and recognize their problems with it. The pharmaceutical company Pfizer carried out a study a number of years ago that found that half of men aged between 40 and 70 suffer from erectile dysfunction. Any friend's spring to mind who come within this huge proportion of men? And within the heterosexual paradigm, the sexual liberation of women has left men in a vulnerable situation comparatively. "Women have also evolved considerably in a sexual sense," said Adrián Sapetti, director of Madrid's Center for Sexology and Psychiatry. "It used to be one size fits all. Now men are faced with women who are more experienced than them and find it intimidating to think of themselves as less accomplished." But then no one discusses the fact, which only widens the gap between our ideas of sex and its actual application. "Any man who hasn't had erectile issues should be seeing a psychiatrist – he's the odd one out," Sapetti told me.

But just as much as being honest in acknowledging problems, I'm just as interested in demanding what one wants, something I myself have been guilty of failing to do. This demand, definitely, has to be a private thing. I won't say 'intimate', just in case. I strongly believe in the need to fight, me more than anyone, against this absurd "duty" with respect to sex, which turns it into more of an obligation, an exam, than something to enjoy.

I must admit that, in this, I've been very pleasantly surprised by certain of my online encounters. It might not be face to face, but people are more and more able to ask for what they want, even if this does include some aggressive usernames like "wannafuck". And there's people for everything: from those who only want to be watched while they drink a glass of wine in the nude to others who want you to come over to their house and, without a word, will give you fellatio, to others who just want a cuddle. And at the far side of things there's the Rothenburg Cannibal – however hair raising that case was, it mustn't be forgotten that there were two people doing what excited them – to the very end.

Even Jesus Christ said "Ask and thou shalt receive." What are we waiting for? Yes, it's easier with the internet because everyone's cards are on the table and in no time someone'll show up who accepts you, along with all your foibles. But it's also true that the dynamics of face-to-face encounters are quite different and the fear that informs our philias and phobias can stop us from getting close to the other. These hiding mechanisms and strategies only pronounce our fear that the other will think we're cockhungry – or the opposite. And so we all end up going through the same motions: blow, penetrate, masturbate and, with any luck, filch. Very few people are daring enough to reveal their true desires, or lack of them, which is another input to the great lie that so many of us believe.

But while I'm on the subject of credulity, maybe the most negative factor of this characteristic of mine hasn't been that I've fallen for lies to do with sexual performance but taking the tenets of the sexual revolution at its proponents' word, as if we were the children in The White Ribbon under the sway of Protestant morals in years leading up to World War I. Have I – without the adult filters of perversion or salvation – accepted the idea that there can be nothing bad in sex, and its consequences? Have I therefore got rid of the motor of transgression, defined by so many philosophers, thinkers and studies as the very seed of excitement? With intimacy eliminated by my not holding back of secrets, with innocence half-deflowered, without the shame or blame that give rise to regret and internal conflict, and with the certainty that sex contains nothing bad, what, then, does my internal journey toward eroticism consist of? Maybe I thought homosexuality was transgressive, and felt disappointed when I turned up and found I was accepted there. So I'm left with asexuality as a space, a refuge, for my eagerness to seek out taboo, or as a refection of the complete neutralization of the opposing forces that lead to the construction of desire? This is why I said that when my mother says I'm an angel a part of me believes her. An angel that managed to annihilate, pretty much unintentionally, its own sexuality.

# TIRAMISU

When I was a teenager I fell head over heels in love. Maybe cinema's to blame, but I have had periods of hopeless romanticism. Or maybe because if you're blind, your other senses grow much sharper. Nowadays I've lost some of this enthusiasm and have put aside the idea of being in a couple as a sine qua non of personal development, though I still wait politely in a "bring me it when you can, please" kind of way. I can't deny that when I've had it I've felt as though I'm in my proper environment and some of my best memories are alongside someone I've been in love with.

For a long time, emotional relationships were the big pending matter for me. The reciprocals, let's say. Why couldn't I get a boyfriend? God, with all the people I saw that had managed to get one... Blaming the gay community's hypersexuality seemed a bit too poor me. My female friends, all of whom are super lovely, are also finding it really difficult, and we don't exactly hang out in gay bars all day every day. There's no lack of interesting people, either, in fact I have difficulties making space in my life for all the people I find fascinating. My inopportune and immature maturity maybe had more to do with it. A child trapped in the body of a 45 year old can be rather stimulating – but an old man trapped in that of an 18 year old wasn't all that inviting I don't think.

Time went by and the expectation began killing me. It was one thing to acknowledge homosexuality and another to practice it. It wasn't a total stripping down, but rather a transition between female and male courtly love. An older guy at college who had a girlfriend (though he showed up ten years later, begging me to go to bed with him), another who had a boyfriend... relationships that couldn't even get started, deeply romantic, in which I managed to get close to them, better never so far as holding hands. "Mateo, enough of your pseudorelationships now," one of my friends said, seeing that I, not in very much need of sex, ended up creating these "unconsummated relationships" in my head; my objects of desire, through no fault of their own, opened themselves up to an unexpected gamut of possible ambiguities and suggestions. I felt to an extent met in this love, and that they could cheat on their partners with me all they wanted, no one would ever have to find out!

My sexualized virginity also exerted a strong magnetic pull on repressed homosexuals. I don't know if the front I put on, so immaculate, so passive, brought about in them an unhealthy curiosity or a balm for their own conflicts. And so I managed these pseudorelationships, and all their ellipses, with relative ease – it would all have sailed past any kind of censor because everything happened between the lines – there was always one official account and one beyond that.

But this obviously wasn't enough and the moment came when I wanted a real boyfriend, and a voice saying, ok, all this knowingness is no way to get yourself a man. The expectations surrounding this minor subject (ooh, yes, sex!) that had been created by the psychologist who told me everything would sort itself out in the heat of a requited love were added on to the natural desires. It was then that I – I've never been one of these "when you're least expecting it" kind of guys – had a day in which I saw very clearly that Niels and I were going to be together. Not an arrow in the heart precisely, but very much a revelation, yes. And the fact he was German helped me reinforce the theory that the cause of my singledom until then had been (nothing to do with me!) the fact that people in Spain have no taste.

What happened was that this very Germanically discreet, very quiet person, who I had in front of me every day, who seemed condemned to play only a secondary role, had performed a sudden and unexpected about-turn that meant, now, I was going to make him mine at all costs. A totally lead role, headline act. In a month we're going out together. Take that!

Our love story (at the risk of sound even more egoist) is one of the loveliest and saddest I know. The lesson was incredibly tough and on such a scale that I think I must still be learning from it. Saving the gory details and saying, in summary, that the mutual fascination was based in the classic principle of opposites attract, Niels and I began going out on the basis of two different lacks: he didn't believe in love and I didn't believe in sex. One showed the other the importance of what they didn't believe in and for a time we both lived in the illusion that we were both great teachers as well as great students. It was like a foreign exchange at school. And it didn't take long for reality to burst in, leading to a serious bust up in both sex and love. Out of class and straight to the principal's office.

Initially, this certainty about our inevitable fate as a couple radically changed my attitude when it came to seduction, erasing both the anxiety to make foreplay bear fruit (which while it lasted was like savoring good wine) and thereby making myself worry less about the sex questions, which became less of an imperative. Niels was really amazing: first of all, he had the patience of a saint. But he also knew how to make me feel wanted and fulfilled even without sex, even as a part of him that had previously been hidden began to emerge, which made every day feel like a victory. I, the great exponent of transparency, now found myself fascinated by his opacity, which had to be thawed out bit by bit.

Niels, once the scales had fallen from his eyes, converted, becoming the most ardent of lovers. He began dropping all the ballasts he'd accumulated – opening up, learning to trust – dazzled by how natural and instinctive our mutual feeling was. I've always been more open to passion and understood as something fairly obvious that this was the path to happiness, began to drive the mechanisms of desire, the sexuality that exists in close up – your favorite square centimeter of skin – and the excitement of a fictitious but full awareness of the person in front of you day after day, practically every hour. Putting myself in the hands of someone who didn't even have to try to arouse me, but simply smell the way he always smelled, be tactile the way he always was, was enough to make me feel ready for pleasure, full of love and generally happy in life. An inexhaustible source that fills up the hours, that changes time's dynamic because the next priorities are light years away and the sense of time passing is no longer what it once was.

Bataille explains it better than anyone: "Without the intimate understanding between two bodies that only grows with time, conjunction is furtive and superficial, unorganised, practically animal and far too quick, and often the expected pleasure fails to come. A taste for constant change is certainly neurotic, and certainly can only lead to frustration after frustration. Habit, on the other hand, is able to deepen the experiences that impatience scorns to bother with.". It turns out that the conservatives weren't wrong after all – just overly rigid in imposing their ideas.

For my part, I was teaching Niels to believe in love and trying to help him reconcile with life in general, but at the same time discovering that it was nothing like what I had imagined or seen in the movies; in fact there was far more to it than I had thought. In this case, it was even better than I could have possibly imagined. It was another train of logic (or illogic), the dynamic of which no one could possibly predict. Sometimes not even those who were generating it. Welcome – after years of idealizing and desiring – to the supercomplicated, superstimulating world of sentimental relations. That good tiramisu – the best in town.

Niels was great when it came to intimacy. I was crazy about his somewhat vulnerable character, which added intensity to life, but he was also gutsy, witty and resourceful. I really thought I'd hit the jackpot. We'd be together forever. His attention to detail, his capacity for hard work, his effort and his determination to become a better person struck me as everyday deeds of heroism. I, lazier and more self indulgent, could do no more than admire his almost Teutonic perfectionism, day after day – I didn't understand that in fact his motivation was a strong self-dislike. And it must also be said that this positive change of attitude and renewed lust for life made me proud – I felt like I was the cause of both. I can now see how my narcissism prevented me from seeing clearly.

On the other side of this (in one way very real) mirage that I still sustain as one of the great treasures of my life journey, faults started to appear... approximately as large and as tectonically active as the San Andreas fault! I began to take backward steps with sex and to see, though I still thought myself capable of enjoying it, it was hardly something that moved me deeply. When we happened to be apart, I missed him, but I didn't miss sex, and then when we saw each other again, it was far from being the first thing on my mind.

Having loosened up so we could get going, seeing myself in the role of ardent lover, after half an hour I was still bored as an oyster. I wanted out as quickly as possible. I don't consider it premature but I do come quickly but don't take too long or my mind will wander, and so I felt truly suffocated on the days when Niels was more inspired and kept on going and going, or after my happiness that he'd ejaculated ("great, it's over", I always thought), he had the good luck to still be hard and ready for round two, never a good thing as far as I was concerned. In other words: I'd reached my sexual plenitude... but that still left me a long way from being a normal person quote unquote. Well then... first obstacle overcome – of not feeling able to enjoy – I came up against the second and possibly greater one: being aware that, in reality, sex didn't seem to me anything to write home about, and I preferred it in small doses.

Linked (or not) to this same process, Niels began to backtrack on his unconditional dedication to love and dusted off his old suspicious attitude, years-deep as he was by that point in a much tougher life than the one I'd had. That's the inconvenient thing about these admirable self-made men: they've learned that if they really want something done well they have to do it themselves, and consider any outside interference suspicious – they feel instantly micromanaged. My view of feelings was more essentialist – he said more savage, but I thought our love was strong enough to withstand the possible risk, whether that of our out of kilter desires or the fact our career ambitions were so similar we were bound to feel like one was doing better than the other. Even his constant suspicion ("one day I'll find your weak point", he'd say) seemed as nothing if it were understood as part of intrinsic insecurity that love, and all its good effects, would be able to alleviate. But I was obviously wrong.

Because it was his first love, Niels couldn't understand that such a love, or other more or less intense versions of the same, could possibly lead to friendship. Though I don't agree with that as an idea, from there everything enters into more normal territory. It shouldn't be forgotten that I'm the overconfident one. Nonetheless, it all turned out horribly and he started coming up with the most bizarre and contradictory theories. Suddenly, in my first ever stable relationship, in his eyes I'd become some kind of Don

Juan teeming with exes desperate to give it another try with me or, what's worse, with those who, now that I felt comfortable enough to have a relationship as God intended (the expression is valid for homosexuals too), wanted round two to restore an honor that had never actually been wounded because, as I've already mentioned, my ascent into sexual relations had been so disastrous. This was one of the trains of thought that really didn't take much for me to leave behind because deep down he knew very well how much I loved him, full stop. I only had to put the brakes on and look him in the eye. Then he saw a truth superior to all of this.

But the second and far more perverse argument that teased our emotional stability was this: Niels used my undervaluation of sex to fuel his paranoia, the idea that I was like a child playing with dynamite, unaware of the destructive potential of what I was doing, and he, of course, would be collateral damage, he'd be in the line of fire and his life in danger. "You have no idea, Mateo, but you actually exude sex." That's that. I couldn't help but laugh, obviously, firstly because considering where I'd come from this was just about the most surreal thing he could say and, further, because courtship is part of what I do and it can't slip through my hands just like that. But there were uglier accusations like "one day you'll find yourself with a dick in your mouth and then you won't be able to say no" which underlined a certain supposition that homosexuality really is all Sodom and Gomorrah. And that really was deeply unamusing. Like anyone who becomes jealous, and he really did become quite pathological, he couldn't understand that two can't fuck if one doesn't want to and that, if it happens anyway, then we're talking about a violation, with me as victim.

When his suspicions came to dominate his behavior altogether, added to the fact I began to travel for my work while he was unemployed (the great emotional drama in Spain today), the ideal ground was prepared for the cultivation of a monster. It meant that, alone and with no one to stop him, he built up a dedicated arsenal of arguments and remarks (he was never lacking in rational intelligence). Our arguments, as well as being unpleasant, became unsustainable and had the physical effect on me of rejection: they made me tremble like a frightened child. I, who had been so happy to find someone who would activate my sexual enjoyment to the extent of my limited abilities, was now going to be accused of being a globetrotting sucker of cocks, because the last thing Niels came at me with was that he'd leave me before I slept with yet another person, because according to him it was bound to happen sooner or later.

This nonsense reached such a pitch that I couldn't help but think Niels had lost it, and that his personal issues were far greater than the periodic crises every couple must go through. It was painful but I took the view, honorably I think, that all of this was really necessary for Niels – for him to open up his wounds little by little and clean them out. I knew full well that the green-eyed monster is terrible and invincible. And I cried oceans that the person I'd been most in love with and whom I tried to give the best of myself had made me his nightmare and the target for all his most ancestral ire. Nowadays, three years after the breakup (we ended up being together for a year and a half, though it felt like a lifetime), he still blanks me on the street. I think he didn't, under any circumstances, want to be introduced to anyone with the cordial title "my ex". I also think he didn't want to come face to face with the one person who could really undermine his conspiracy theories, or face up to the fact he boycotted our happiness. "I look at you and I know you love me," he said when we were together, "but then I can't get my head around why you go and do all these things." And if he looked at me again, again his reasoning would be disarmed.

Underneath the more obvious interpretations there was a more bitter depth. "Uttering a new word is what people fear most" says Dostoyevsky at the beginning of Crime and Punishment. For Niels that word was happiness, which brought about more instability in him than the adversity he'd grown accustomed to dealing with in his life. Whatever the case, there it went, as though someone had flushed it down the toilet: my ideal notion that love can conquer and cure all. I understood for the first time my eagerness to make people around me feel good and to disseminate positive ideas as something counterproductive, and I half took on the idea (I still find it difficult to believe) that time might not put things in their rightful place and that I will always be a hateful person in his eyes even though everything I did was in good faith. That's all. The great love of my life. Which part of his split personality was real? Bataille: "There is nothing really illusory in the truth of love; the beloved being is indeed equated... with the truth of experience.

Chance may will it that through that being, the world's complexities laid aside, the lover may perceive the true deeps of existence and their simplicity." And for as long as our passion lasted, this was absolutely the case.

But even in this apparent letting myself off the hook for the breakup – saying Niels initiated everything, good and bad – there's still a part of me that connects his sudden fits of rage with my problematic sexuality. Niels said that I "would ruin anyone's self esteem" and, somehow and although he was referring to my totally predatory ego, it did prompt me to think that my oppressive sexuality must have had something to do with the erosion of his self esteem (however much he might have picked holes in himself); oppressive, not always willing and at times clogged up. So we come back round the question about whether there's anyone with sufficient emotional maturity to understand that my sexual aloofness isn't to the detriment of my love for that person, and neither is it actually linked to his inability to satisfy me. And of course the fact-checking likely to be prompted in anyone already carrying insecurities can be just the spark for the finale dynamite. Were Niels' jealousies, if not justified, at least understandable? In any case, I began to infer the true drama of asexuality: its possible incompatibility with a solid emotional relationship. The factor that sooner or later would bring about watchfulness, undermine confidence or, even if that didn't happen, simply make the other person feel fed up, prey to thoughts of a possibly greater satisfaction elsewhere.

I took two morals from this 'sexed' reading of our relationship: one that left me in a very bad place, which was that you can't take something on that you don't like merely to please your lover. For good and for ill, the generation of martyrs has had its day. The other, far finer but just as awkward: if someone is even just a little bit empathic, they can't really enjoy sex if their partner isn't enjoying it equally. On that point Niels turned out to be lucky, though he ended up focusing on it too self-destructively, almost miserably.

I don't know whether because of maturity, unawareness of lack of empathy, but I certainly never thought Niels would leave me in search of someone who was more sexually active. I felt confident he'd be faithful. So I suppose neither of us labored particularly hard to empathize. The conclusion that I come to is that I always though he'd think like I do – and vice versa. And that's why I though the problems were relative, that his faithfulness was in good health and that sex wasn't the be all and end all. That really we were a great couple. But he was living in a hell of constant red alert, riddled with half-truths and hidden motives. Without coming to believe that I would be sexually satisfied and that I didn't have to add to the defeat of my enormous ego seducing everything that moved. That was why I went to discos, "waging war" as he put it.

Our polar opposites meat that the image one projected on the other became its antithesis: I, fairly logical and dependable (I have other faults) became pure uncertainty for Niels, and he, with his volcano constantly about to explode, became a sweet, dear little lamb. A phone call from Brazil was the straw that broke the camel's back. Niels couldn't stand it any more and he left me. "You're destroying me," he said. And so I came round most brutally to a reality – my reality – just as self-created and slippery as Niels', only at the opposite pole... Damn poles!

After the breakup, Niels reminded me of a time when we were talking about infidelity and I admitted that if it came down to him saying he needed more sex than I could offer, I'd almost find it a relief to delegate his satisfaction to someone else. I really am a hapless idiot – this kind of thing should never be said, or, in any case, if he wasn't satisfied (something he always denied), he should have been the one putting forward such an idea. But it was on my mind, so (stupidly, I repeat) I let him know. He told me he didn't want to be with someone who was like that. And that he didn't like my values (in relation to this and several other things). And he dropped in the fact – and this was when I realized he was going all out to hurt me – that in the three months since we'd broken up he'd been with numerous men who were technically far more accomplished than me. I expected something like that might come, but just because I'd expected it didn't make it hurt any less. I began to cry immediately, registering how vulnerable I was on that front and that our past intimacy made for numerous weak spots into which he could stick his finger all he liked, gloating over my pain. At that time Niels was oscillating between "you've destroyed my life" and "I'll never find another like you", made up for it with a "but I enjoyed it more with you, just in a different way." Which of the two Nielses to listen to? For the sake of my sanity – just about all I had left at that point – I decided to listen to the more hurtful, thereby enabling myself to get away from someone who, paradoxically, had revealed moments of boundless happiness.

I suppose we all carry around a certain amount of emotional trauma or at least that we're never the same again after a deep relationship ends. In my case, Niels' victory over me made me doubt whether someone like "good Niels" really existed who didn't also have in him the "bad Niels". I was erring away from the idea that the person I'd loved had changed and more toward the idea that he'd disappeared altogether, been substituted by a villainous and fairly caricature-ish villain. A little bit too Swan Lake, I know. Or maybe too Bataille, because now I read this, which I believe Niels swallowed hook line and sinker: "We ought never to forget that in spite of the bliss, love promises its first effect is one of turmoil and distress... Passion fulfilled itself provokes such violent agitation that the happiness involved, before being a happiness to be enjoyed, is so great as to be more like its opposite, suffering... Love reiterates: "If only you possessed the beloved one, your soul sick with loneliness would be one with the soul of the beloved". Partially at least this promise is a fraud. But in love the idea of such a union takes shape with frantic intensity, though differently perhaps for each for each of the lovers" And frantic is what it was. Me wanting to control the uncontrollable. We didn't do badly, we lasted a decent amount of time. After all the drama, he decided to turn a new page, open a new account, and went back to Berlin.

I haven't yet been in another stable relationship. My hopefulness comes back relatively quickly, but usually goes away again just as fast. Since Niels and I finished, bad as it might be for me to admit (if Niels knew he'd feel totally vindicated), something in me has changed. In spite of everything, I believe it bolstered me in terms of my capacity to be liked by someone and to cohabit. I'm a likable guy, and that's clearly important for first impressions. It's true as well that I'm developing new skills all the time through my work, and my passion for all different kinds of people continues to increase. I've gone from being the self-denying harvester of snubs to finding it fairly easy to meet interesting people, people with whom there's sometimes chemistry and with whom, in a more or less fluid manner, might turn into a relationship project.

Alberto was the first guy with whom I had an emotional bond following the hurricane. Good looking, intelligent and a decent person. Though he had a bit of a bland side to him, actually we had a great time. We'd been together for three weeks, not much at all, and I began to have premonitions as I had in my previous relationship, but the inverse: it wasn't going to work and that was that. It was really difficult to explain it to him and, in fact, up until a few days ago I hadn't managed to express it like this to his face.

Alberto, who is now a more than amicable ex, someone with whom I always like, above all, to converse, taught me a lot about negotiating sex. Long story short, he immediately told me what he liked and what he didn't and I didn't quite know how to meet him on that level and just say: sex, in general, I'm not really that into it. In the past, I've really tried to keep up in this respect and I am to blame for effectively making the other person's decision for them: presupposing that the other is going to see it as unsustainable, and get out as fast as they can. I think he's right in part. He said he didn't remember the sex being a problem with us and assured me that as long as I set it out right from the start, openly, he was sure that I'd find ways of making it work, or people who would at least be happy to give it a go. He accused me of the thing I accused Niels of: self boycott. And recently I've begun to admit not only to close friends about my virtually constant lack of sexual appetite, but also to people I'm only flirting with. This book is the culmination of the process.

I still haven't dared admit it to anyone I'm really into, because then I get really worried they're going to run a mile and I prefer to wait until they're at least somewhat emotionally involved (how Machiavellian it all seems) before starting up this particular mill. But Alberto insists: this mill really isn't a mill, and let him without sin cast the first stone. Could he be right? He also said he thought I suffered from pregnancy syndrome but the inverse: instead of thinking everyone I see is a loser – or in my case, asexuals on a grand scale – all I see is highly sexed people, when there must be one or two out there who don't need that much sex. Am I a sexual hypochondriac? Maybe. Strangely, I've come across some real sex machines in my life... perhaps the laws of attraction have meant that I unconsciously looked for them or that unconsciously they found their way to me. Everything's so complicated.

In theory, the reasoning behind the watermill idea and the pregnancy seems very solid to me. And I have an experience that backs it up: I surprised myself once when, having pursued (almost harassed) a guy named Luis, who I'd liked a lot for six months, the triumphant moment finally arrived in which, having come close to victory a number of times, we kissed and spent the night together, and like an idiot I fell asleep in the middle of us having sex. I was a little bit drunk but the thing was that he didn't talk at all while we were having sex and that, added to my tendency to get bored in these situations, led to this tragic ending. But Luis, harking back to that night, described it as "very lovely" and I didn't detect in him the slightest irony or reproach – though in a second foolhardy attempt it didn't work out well and we decided to leave it, this time by a process of elimination, deciding that to put ourselves in Morpheus' hands was the best option. My mind wanted to believe in the possible restructuring of what is considered to be a couple. I did, to an extent, discard the possibility of meeting someone with the exact same levels of desire as me. But not the possibility of meeting someone who could understand and separate the two – who could reach the core point, which is no doubting the love purely on the basis of the sex. And, above all, that that person renounce or simply not aspire to the apparent ecstasy of uniting the two. A modern person, yes, someone truly able to disattach from centuries of relationships based on the idea that you have to get everything from a relationship – that your partner has to be able to fulfill you in every respect, and you them. It's commonly said that relationships are about sacrifices, but I don't see why that shouldn't go for sex as well. Surely there are a lot of couples who don't have sex and are still together – I don't know if as richly – but nonetheless joined by the many things they do share, and I'm not talking only about practical, logistical things.

Nonetheless, then Alfonso springs to mind – and then everything comes tumbling down. It's a tale that, I'm perfectly aware, still troubles me every time I think about it. What happened? Well, he seemed to be totally perfect and we got on really well, but in the three weeks we were together I didn't get even a semi – to his considerable distress, and to mine. And I don't even mean we managed to get it going a little bit. I mean nada!

Fun, caring, decent person, intelligent, good looking... all the boxes you'd want ticked in terms of someone to meet the parents and someone you'd be proud to be with in front of your friends. And we had real intimacy. We were alike in ways so improbable that they made you believe in divine intervention, destiny's magic halo. But there was no way. He always said it was fine, that with me he didn't need more than I was giving him. But I didn't believe him. It is true that I began to detect a certain tendency to dependence in him, to understanding love as some kind of salvation, and that, coming from where I was coming from, put me off. But it's equally as true that when I see Alfonso I think: "this guy still likes me and I love being with him. We could be happy together." He must think me a super awkward customer, though I know that something in him reconciles itself with me every time we meet. There's a spark.

It's the only case I'm genuinely unsure if I was right about, and I sometimes kick myself for not having tried harder. It was also the only time I really thought about imposing a "separation of powers": sex on one side and love on the other. The thing is, yes, I have the foresight that, even if he agreed, the thing was sure to be an emotional nailbomb in his wellbeing and probably mine too. It makes me wonder, is there anyone really capable of honestly renouncing sex with their partner – excluding clinical cases, which demand strict consent – without, deep down, hoping that something might change? I don't know. It reminds me of people (and myself, in certain moments) who, love-drunk, accept an emotional companion who says he only wants to fuck every now and then, though they aren't actually prepared for a relationship of that kind... but whom they try to trap and, sooner or later, put a ring on their finger, weaving a patient and, often, humiliating, web. Settling, in other words, for what they want to give. Begging for something that's sheer nonsense unless given willingly, without pressure or scheming. In any case I don't want to be that guy who thinks that just putting all his cards on the table strips him of responsibility. At least not when I'm aware of the mechanisms of self-deception that, more or less, we've all applied from time to time.

So I return to the lament – oh! – the sexual always overlaps with the moral. I note that something in me feels a little dangerous, a little wounding. Which is why I've recently retraced my steps and begun in the opposite direction: instead of imbibing coffee via the tiramisu, I'm drinking them all at once, in single gulps, not even stopping for air. Ready, steady... go!

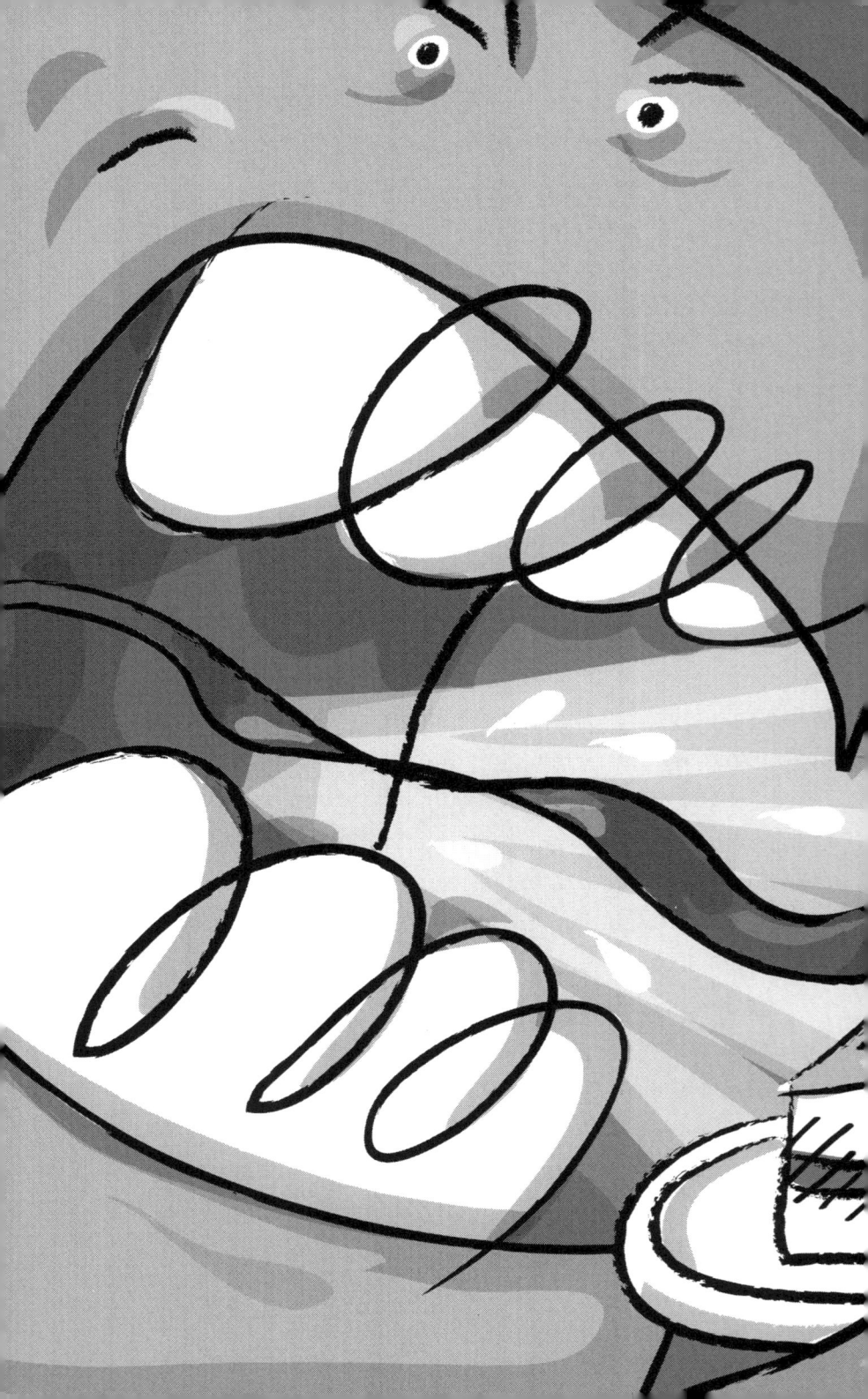

# THE PROMISCUITY OF THE ASEXUAL

After a guest on the famous "Tonight We Cross the Missis-sipi" program was asked a question, I asked my mother: what's a nymphomaniac? To the quick interpretation "sex addict" my mother also added: "but it's because deep down they aren't satis-fied that they want more and more." Expert in hard-to-substan-tiate theories, as ever. But I think I've inherited a bit of this: the thought-provoking aspect of an idea is always more appealing to me than its factual element and something of this, I'm sure, mo-ves through what I'm writing here.

I'm obviously far from being a nympho, but this comment of my mother's has come back to me many times; I remember her saying very clearly, with the radio in her bathroom playing the legendary Luis del Olmo. The caprices of memory. And, though I struggled to spark my sexual engine until the age of 21, I myself have been this seeker of thrills that will never come. It isn't a compulsive search, but almost. Not so much in quality as in variety. And so, sure enough, doubt takes over me: does the sexual hyperactivity flaunted by so many actually have the same origin as my own?

On the one hand, Anthony F. Bogaert said in his 2004 study that "for a variety of reasons - one's attraction to men or women - overt sexual behavior or sexual self-identification may have a less-than-perfect correspondence" and he spoke of asexuals as often having "a certain level of sexual activity, maybe as the result of trying things out or maybe to please their partner."

Having explained the latter, now for the former. The thing that's prompted my female friends to say on more than one occasion: "For an asexual, you get a loot of sex – more than us!" And, definitely, for me the great tyranny of sex is that, though I've gone through everything that's involved with accepting it isn't really my thing, I never lose hope that I might one day meet the man who strikes all thoughts of asexuality from my mind and turns out to be the fuck of the century. I am, as Pasolini said of God, an atheist with a nostalgia for belief. And Bataille was spot on in saying " it can happen that unless we see that transgression is taking place we no longer have the feeling of freedom that the full accomplishment of the sexual act demands - so much so that a scabrous situation is sometimes necessary to a blase individual for him to reach the peak of enjoyment.".

Having also explained that I find sex neither invasive nor disagreeable (though there are people who certainly are both – best simply steered clear of) I sometimes say to myself: "well, no harm in trying." Not exactly that I let chance to enter in to my sexual dynamic, because it all still ends up being far more devised than this might make it seem. Simply, yes, I've gone through deliberations, reasoning and the emotional wear and tear of accepting that a "if they catch you here they'll kill you" is a low price to pay compared with winning the lottery of meeting the kind of man who makes me squeal. The sensation of medical consultation that I get sometimes with sex sometimes has become a kind of general checkup with various specialists to see if I can worked out the origins of the symptoms. Or maybe a looking over by different doctors with the same specialism until they give me the diagnosis I want to hear. It could also be thought of as applying to sex Pascal's discussion of the theoretical probability of God's existence. Pascal sought to demonstrate God's existence by applying to theology the reasoning that governs decisionmaking. He argued that if God didn't exist, it would make no difference not to believe in Him. If He did exist, not believing would damn you for eternity, but to believe meant the promise of salvation. Given that salvation is preferable to condemnation (the greatest gain, in probability terms), it's more practical to act as though God exists, just in case. If not a nostalgia for belief, leave the door open to the possibility that I'm all wrong in my sexual agnosticism.

So, little by little, and in rather Pascalian terms, I've gone along sporadically familiarizing myself with sex. To begin with it felt very alien, but the day came when I said: it's OK, you can perform now to a decent level, and you're capable of disconnecting and reflecting more now too. So we cross "sex for sex's sake" off the list. Done. Conclusion? Yet another letdown. For all that I've felt excitement and "measured up" like any other person in a number of different situations. Once more, then, the contradiction between thought and deed. Disdain has made me force my own limits sometimes and to expose myself to situations that bring me closer to (my mother's version) of nymphomania than to having the sexual life of your average citizen. In this conquest of excitement, emotion disasters have led me both to flirt with sordidness and to knowing, over and above any advantages, the disadvantages of a more out-there kind of sex, to the point of being an asexual who caught crabs from a French journalist during a heavy petting session in the Venice Lido. So much glamour can't be a good thing...

I joined the gym in 2011, to the surprise of many people given the fact sport and I have never gotten along very well. But there, though not right from the beginning, a new front opened up: that of contact with the male body en masse, with nudity and the vanity not only of gays but of heterosexuals too. In short, a lot of strutting and preening, a chance for voyeurs and exhibitionists both to give free reign to their fantasies. This was also where I thought perhaps the transgressive sensation might be resuscitated. Only to be let down again. Heterosexuals are only too happy to be looked at, which made that transgression vanish immediately. Designed with almost periscopic halls of mirrors that mean you don't have to even move to get an eyeful, in this back and forth of gazes that I thought all came no strings attached (mainly because everyone was at it), one day I had an encounter in the showers with a very good looking guy with whom I'd exchanged abdominal-to-abdominal glances that one could simply have attributed to mutual affirmation. When he caught me gawping at him, naked as the day he was born, he took the next step and invited me into his shower cubicle. After being initially disconcerted – neither shy nor lazy, not I – I went into his cubicle as if this were the most normal thing in the world. Forgetting to say "Why thank you, sir."

Between him kneeling down and me ejaculating no more than two liters of water can have passed through that shower. I struck me later on that his boyfriend must have been finishing wailing on his abs and about to show up, and that was why the guy went so quickly with me and asked for "dispersal" to avoid any problems. Fine, great by me. I was feeling gobsmacked when I got to work. Somehow, and given that this had all happened at 9am, it seemed like a dream. It had been so like a porn film that for a moment I thought of looking for the remote control to rewind it and watch the scene again. We've met since then and, yes, spoken in a more relaxed manner. He told me he ran a restaurant.

"We have to find out which one!" said my girlfriends. I said: "I chose not to ask, I don't want to be invasive." Their quite logical response was to say it was slightly more invasive going in his cubicle. But things run in reverse in these cases: sex is not intimate, and finding out run-of-the-mill formalities like name and occupation is startling.

My gymnasium adventure then turned into its own antithesis. When I was researching my article on sex and blind people, one of the most surprising results was that, for them, with touch being one of their most important senses, a rotund or flaccid body was much more exciting than the marble-hewn-sixpack-and-bulging-biceps kind of beauty we're so used to, an idea that led me in a new direction: that of bears – that sweet, rotund collective nonetheless a priori so physically unattractive to me. The chosen one was fairly goodlooking and clever but, to be honest, he had a fairly massive belly. I liked feeling all that weight on top of me. He had a certain something and I was pleasantly surprised early on, I think because of something as pathetic as the fact that being crushed created an effect on me similar to passion. But everything else was the same and, what's more, this guy – who later confessed to me that he worked occasionally for a senior official in Spain's Partido Popular, get this – was like a bear with a sore head the morning after. By the second time, I'd had more than enough.

And the last experience I had that is relevant in this discussion of transgression was when I went home with an Opus Dei sympathizer. He was pretty unattractive physically, but I was kind of turned on by the whole holier-than-thou thing. When I came out with one of my classic "everything's pointing to sex but in the end I'll slip away" he said something along the lines of "I'll try and see your side, even though our ways of thinking are so different" (which was a good summary of the bidirectional logic of the situation) and took his shirt of, revealing his huge Sacred Family medallion. Since he didn't like kissing and wanted, above all, to give it, and I didn't on that particular night feel like taking it, we ended up fondling and that was about all. Chastity won out. The next day he got up to go to work and I pretended to be tired and that was the end of that. Amen.

Failing to find men that excited me, I sought to place them in exciting contexts. After all, my first sexual encounter (though not the time I lost my virginity) was with a friend of my brother's who managed to overcome my resistance by the mere fact that he considered himself straight. The only words he said were "you're circumcised" and "I think I prefer chicks." A deeply sensitive guy.

One of the most revealing aspects of Dr. Bogaert's study was that within the thousands of categories into which the sexual terrain can be divided, there is one based on two extremely interesting concepts: receptive and proceptive sexuality. The proceptive is the more obvious: this is the part that impels a person to find someone with whom to vent the sexual desire. But the receptive – more associated with the feminine – is based on "the capacity to be provoked by the meeting of certain sexual conditions whose satisfaction isn't all that linked to the act of sex in itself." On hearing this, I thought hallelujah! Now we're getting somewhere. In the receptive category, also linked with a more plastic vision of the sexual, desire and attraction aren't necessarily one and the same. Desire is projection. Attraction is moving closer. How many times have I become super flirty only to later on – once we're in bed, once the context has changed, the situation evaporated or ceased to seem new and exciting – not wanted to do it anymore? And I say: a shit load of times. And how many times, when I've recounted what I've been through, have people said commented that I have a very feminine perspective on sex? Ditto.

Which means it isn't strange that, during a time in which I've wanted to be footloose and uninhibited, I've become quite familiar with seeing my sexual impetus come up but then fade, my penis rebel and the whole thing trickier than using a butter knife to cut through whale skin. In the preamble conversations, in which I don't in fact draw attention away from what's coming, but generally try to give a brief synopsis of my relationship with sex, the vast majority of the responses are sighs loosed into the air like stray bullets that, sometimes, have hooked the other person more strongly than if I'd offered unconditional sex. As if sex's supposed superpotency is unmasked, making it open season for people to reveal their own vulnerabilities, unguardedly, and a strange sense of intimacy arises. It really has led to very emotional moments that have made me ask myself whether, in such an athletic sexual dynamic, what I offer becomes a kind of discovery, some special opportunity for them to have different kinds of nights in which they can play a different character. But these encounter can sometimes be a little surreal as well.

To highlight a couple of examples, I remember this German director who didn't mind not being able to consummate the act because he actually had a boyfriend who didn't like kissing so all he was after was affection. After a lovely evening spent chatting in the nude and him telling me about his troubled relationship with his stepfather, he ended up writing him a letter whilst the two of us had breakfast. Another example was the guy from Madrid who, after we'd watched the film Lola Montes (which augured intensity) and having (within my limits) had pretty decent sex, broke down, crying on my chest after telling me about his hugely varied life, which included a heterosexual wife and an unwell mother. He wasn't much of a talker, and was so delicate and sincere but also hard to get close to.

Lastly, though this one is a serial lover, there is also the case of the sociologist who, to begin with, offered to give me classes in sex to remove me from this lack of appetite – which he wasn't convinced by. And then he got into an open relationship with someone else, and it became particularly difficult for him to see me. When we had caresses rather than full sex he totally lost it and said he though this really wasn't good – really, really not good. Mortal sin. Once, though it was clear I wasn't going to give him the sex he wanted, he sniffed his Poppers anyway, this being part of his usual ritual – a way of convincing himself that our non-sex was "just sex". He passed me the bottle and, though it made no sense (given that I've never touched a single drug my whole life), I sniffed a little, though it didn't effect me in the slightest. "You always violate me" he'd say, because I always somehow appealed to the most affectionate part of him.

But anyway, although the spirit of this somewhat Chestertonian paradox doesn't bother me, I see very well that it continues giving shape to something I definitely don't like. The reality is, I haven't accepted it. It's strange, but as a gay it's always made me proud to bear it as if it were the most natural thing in the world, come what may. Little by little people at my work, my family, friends, even strangers came to know about it, and at the same time I was learning to deliver it with less and less ado – more elegantly. My aim was always to not be defined by my gayness, and though it's been difficult I believe I've achieved that at least. One day, during the most conflicted part of the process, I remember saying to my father, in one of the most serious conversations I've had with him my whole life, that I felt that I had failed in my intention to avoid my homosexuality defining me. Faced with such drama, my poor father felt a little alarmed and then he and my mother suggested it might be better for me to spend my summers not back home but in Madrid, I might be happier staying in my milieu, my routine. And they were right on point, really, given that my homosexuality has always weighed more on me in that place. It wasn't so much the times (always pretty mindblowing to me) when people I'd never met in my life screamed insults at me in the street as the sensation that there, in my home town, life's important things simply couldn't occur – I had a general feeling of the brakes being slammed on. Impatience, for me, generates a lot of anxiety. Over time I've managed to rid my trips there of this stigma – I once even had a more than acceptable "rustic" affair. But this asexuality thing, although as I've already said it isn't something people "pick up on" in the street, meets far greater resistance in me than I ever found with homosexuality.

I'm afraid that sometimes one must accept that there's a part of oneself that one doesn't feel proud about, an Achilles heel contained in this constant desire to get as close to what one would like to be. I don't like the feeling of realizing that, contrary to what I've always thought – from skipping ropes with the girls at elementary school to learning the Oscars by heart because both seemed like more fun than anything my town had to offer – I actually don't like being different. I actually don't even know how to be.

A friend once said he'd never had any problem with being gay until he met other gays. This needs to be taken with a pinch of salt; clearly, the fact that sometimes gays like the opportunity to be among our "own kind" because it means we can be critical of gays without straying into homophobia. I wanted to be one of these "cut from a different cloth" homosexuals too, without acknowledging how protected I also felt to be part of a collective. Indeed, without your more stereotypical gays, it would have fallen to the more "refined" among us to step up and take the lead, and I don't think we would have been able to deal with that. Aside from highminded discussions of art cinema, we're not good for much.

Never as a homosexual did I force myself toward heterosexuality in the same way that asexuality has made me explore sexuality. A man who likes men but refuses to undergo the life changes this implies (which are becoming less and less) and lets himself be carried along by social norms and only have intimacy with women – this has always seemed like a betrayal to me, a kind of violence. A huge deception, as I see it. But then I've also had moments when I, confounded by circumstances, or when I encounter the small number of women who do turn me on, see myself in a less forced, unnatural way, thinking about diving in with said girl. Self indulgence?

In terms of my asexuality, the struggle has been far more bloody. The good thing is that it's been carried out with myself alone – no one else has been hurt – although this might be the real motive given that there are things one does for others before oneself. The only impostor, in any case, is me, and there's only a certain point one can work against oneself until. But why do I embark on actions that are so contrary to my desires, or, rather, my non desire? As part of the Psychology module at my University we made a presentation on a rape in a school and the reactions of the parents, the children and the teachers. I had to play the role of the headteacher at the school and, when one of my peers, in the role of one of the fathers, said it couldn't have been his child because he was gay, my response was that it could have been an act of rejecting his own nature. Our teacher laughed and, though he applauded the "performance", said I'd been watching too many movies. Fine, my life might be a movie now, I've been acting as though it is for a few months now anyway.

Do we accept non-acceptance, then? This is the greatest drama, almost more so than the tricky emotional combination. I thought I could be an outsider without any problems – that my character was sufficiently robust. But thus far all I've managed is membership of well recognized outsider groups – the intellectual weirdo collective, the faggots-mostaffected. And now, in spite of Bogaert and his studies, in spite of all these unsatisfied women alongside their caged husbands, I see no mirror in which to look at myself and recognize anything. I didn't know I wanted so much to be part of a group, but can only conclude that this is in fact the case. Not having done it with drugs or fashion, I end up succumbing to sex not because people say I'm supposed to, but because of the way I feel without it. My friends see advances in me now that I'm in a time of being uninhibited, but really the opposite is the case. And this book, at its very core, hopes to create nothing less than a current of opinion that generates a movement that will make me feel less alone. And that's as far as self-compassion goes. End.

# WE

# TIME AND DESIRE

As this coming to grips with asexuality turned from an essay into something far more autobiographical, my brother drew my attention to how premature and inconclusive it is to speak of the hardships of desire at the age of twenty eight – which used to be an age at which you could still easily be a virgin. He was probably right. But I – half-adult ahead of my time, half-eternal child – have always had a bad time with timing, with the idea of there being a right and a wrong time for anything.

It's my mother's fault – in the least negative sense of the word – because of the fact she always treated us like adults. Or at least beings no less infantile than her – she was at times like an older sister to us. This is why I've always gone against ideas that simplify the suffering, decision-making capacities and complexity of children. I remember thinking on an outing in the countryside at nine years old when I felt an allergic reaction coming on: "How is it possible for me to be allergic now if I haven't been my whole life?" We forget that, from birth, we have this strange sensation that we've always been around. Our infancy, or whatever you want to call it, gets lost on the horizon and this means that the space our brains have for the past becomes smaller and smaller. It's always the same – the distance we're at makes no difference because memories only become hidden as we move forward. The earth is round but memories, even of one's own life, are as well.

Which is why it's more than possible to feel existential fatigue at nine years old and the urgency of an everlasting condemnation when the body suggests it to us. This unease, this uncertainty, this anguish – all more or less justified – take on a complexity sufficient that, in their playing out, they become worth the writing of a whole book. This one, for example.

When it's come to analyzing my sexuality I've felt the same thing: although seven years might not be a lot to base conclusions on (the last man I went to bed with said that, being himself 40 years in, he felt his sexuality had fluctuated considerably) I might be goaded by the sheer urgency of someone bringing this issue to light, be it as it may someone who's only had one proper boyfriend and is maybe just a bit dazzled – and has been for a number of years – by the idea that he doesn't like sex. And that's despite the fact it isn't such a sure thing any more that sex is the reserve of youth, nor this myth that a man's sexual zenith is at 18 years old (fingers crossed this is wrong!) – how stupid! I have no desire to focus on this in a nostalgic or a decadent way – the whole "the train's come and gone" or the elegy to the strange purity of burning youth. I don't really even want to draw conclusions. I prefer, even from a confused perspective, the set down every single speck of the energy, of the splendour of being the age I am now.

What I want to say, without under- or overstating it, is that in spite of a sexual problematic with which I struggle constantly, I am nonetheless a content person. However much the search is at times unsettling, it never eclipses my capacity to enjoy other areas of my life and is quite compatible with feelings of being in my prime. And I wouldn't want the passage of time to make me forget that, in my life today, I still have a special ability to make pleasure the axis on which my life turns. But then I suppose it makes sense to ask, what came first? Is it chicken or egg? Have my hedonistic tendencies come to compensate for my inability to enjoy the pleasure of the flesh? Or did the color drain from the flesh before my life became a sequence of gatherings and celebrations? My asexual condition in principle clashes with that of me as lifelover, enthusiast, social animal. I have a friend whose boyfriend says that people say I know how to get the most out of life. That no one thinks of me as a cranky Malvolio, and I don't think anyone has ever said that I'm in need of the famed and ever-distant fuck.

In terms of what I was saying about my mother's treatment of her children, by way of illustration, when I was eight she asked the school psychologist to do some IQ tests on me. They're quite outmoded now in that they only consider this one aspect of the intellect. Little Mateo was sufficiently witty that his mother – who naturally overestimated her children – thought he was extremely gifted. Maybe I was wasting my talents, maybe I needed a new approach to get the best out of me. The results were average to high. I hardly smashed it, but the psychologist said I could, if my parents wanted, go to a school for cleverer children. They – and I'll appreciate this as long as I live – didn't give in to the pride of having a robot boy, and let me decide. And then I made what I consider to be the wisest choice in my life: I opted to carry on feeling less than challenged at school and thereby have less stress. I was only young but I understood fully that this meant I wouldn't get further than everyone else, but rather arrive before them and be able to enjoy the extra time.

I relied particularly heavily on these skills of mine when I arrived in Madrid at eighteen to go to university. The enthusiasm of waking up to life went hand in hand with my desires becoming reality startlingly easily, like some crazy loop of Aladdin's lamp after Aladdin's lamp, its conjurings strung out to infinity... although desire in the singular continued to put up resistance. My positive attitude seems obscene, and for some of those around me that's exactly what it's been (they've told me in no uncertain terms), but I'd be lying if I put it any other way. To me it seems more obscene to take on the role of victim through which so many people try to give weight to their problems. There's no way for me to hide my hopefulness: Madrid and its people have given me something that I'd also forsaken, which is roots, a sense of home. Anyone who forged these in the normal way, in their early years in the place they happened to grow up, can never know how great it is to encounter, however late, a place that neutralizes your sense of rootlessness.

Going from being an outsider to finding yourself around endless people you feel like chatting to, or going to a party or on holiday with, was like some impassioned social stripping away. Without wanting to come across all spiritual, this passion of mine for people – aside from with my true friends – has nonetheless not brought me peace, because I continue to meet endless numbers of super interesting people in this city every day. My enjoyment of both people's depths and surfaces has led me to consider a show of warmth and emotion – not always the usual thing when meeting a stranger – as an essential in the cordiality stakes – something that I know gets on some people's nerves but has also provoked grateful responses, moments of luck and coincidence, more than sufficient compensation for the rest. A bit like Tom Ripley or the Frank Abagnale of Catch Me if You Can, but without such a murky ending, but rather that my day to day becomes a little less unpleasant. And so, life has gifted me a month in a free house in New York on behalf of two friends who I adore, and it's got me to stay in in Berlin, a place I've always wanted to go. People with whom I had a connection and am now friends, but who reached out to me on their own account with no guarantees on my part. People who have made me believe in people, helped me hold on to the innocence of assuming that others might also be innocent. Just as my mother treated my siblings and I like adults and found in us a kind of longing to live up to her expectations, I can say for certain that when you treat people as though they are kind, more than likely they will respond with kindness. They don't want to let you down. And, in any case, I still prefer to be wrong and go through a letdown than assume the worst of someone who in fact had good intentions. This modus operandi has an awful lot to do with the fact these words are being written in a small house on a Greek island belonging to a man who only asks that I look after the plants and whom I don't really even know. Mateo's cushy numbers, as my friends say. Either that or the rewards of an attitude, of believing that, actually, people are amazing.

The point I want to make is that, really, in this exchange of smiles between life and Mateo, the absence of a full enjoyment of my sexuality, this conflict that from time to time sounds so dramatic – including when I read what I've written here – diminishes as a factor in my overall life dynamic when put alongside all the other things that make me feel good, falling down my list of priorities but also (in general) my worries. Life simply becomes something else. Something magnificent – in which I really don't notice some terrible lack. And I see so many people unable to enjoy what they have to hand and how much I value each and every day so much that there are moments when roles reverse and then I see around me people who are truly "frigid" in spirit. Am I transcending yet?!

Neither can I imagine what life would be like for someone who, as well as not enjoying their milieu and not having the luck of such good friends as me, also misfires with something as basic as sex. For me it's like a little extra, take it or leave it. And like a bonus, if you get it you waste it anyway, and if not, you make do. At least that's how I see it from the point I'm at now in my life. Maybe when I'm sixty five, if things aren't going so well and my frustrations start building up, the sense of sexual orphanhood will be reinforced and grow worse to the point that it might even become the epicentre of my emotional earthquake. And that's when I'll write part 2 of my 'On Asexuality', this time as Greek tragedy rather than medieval, magically-inflected fable. For now I feel lucky in all other areas, which takes a lot of the force out of this admittedly thorny subject. And once more, Bataille upbraids the usual thinking when he says "but if good luck favors us, the thing we desire most ardently is the most likely to drag us into wild extravagance and ruin us".

What ruin awaits me? The tongue twister that is desiring desire? Because isn't the distinction between desires and Desire strange? What is the difference between certain desires and others? As I've already said, I feel that all my desires are fulfilled. But only the ones that can be defined, I fear, because sexual desire has something about it that sets it apart. Something that both contradicts all the others and generates them like a father – a father that doesn't lead by example, given that he doesn't correspond to any definition. In fact, it even sometimes goes against what you wants to desire... and can even make you undesirable.

# INSIDE OUT

I went to Paris in 1996 to my aunt's house to learn French, though in the end I learned more cinema than anything else, being so bored that I read the Oscars encyclopedia twice through. It was the summer and around that time Claudette Colbert died, the actress who only ever allowed herself to be shot from one side even though she'd been huge in Hollywood in the 1930's. On French radio they pointed out that she hadn't written an autobiography because she felt her life had been so happy that it couldn't possibly be of interest to anyone. Those were the days when I could still speak and understand French, by the way.

That idea stuck with me far better, obviously, than le passé composé, and still makes me wonder. Why hasn't happiness been a great muse? Much has been written on ways of achieving it, and it often forms the climax in a story... but rarely is that mood treated ecstatically or in any depth. In The Hours Meryl Streep said that one day she thought that that instant in which she felt happy would be the beginning of her happiness, not realizing that happiness was in fact only that moment. Though I consider the film a masterpiece I don't agree with that particular observation – I think happiness is all about perspective. It is hugely complex, for all that people have tried to associate it with naivety or new age nonsense.

In the play Santo, whose three brief parts were written by Ernesto Caballero, Ignacio García May and Ignacio del Moral, I remember the writers saying they wanted to work against the idea that kindness is overrated. "People who think kindness is overrated should be locked in the basement with a psychopath and an axe for company," Aitana Sánchez-Gijón said about the staging. Which prompted me to think that something quite similar happens with happiness. In fact in all my talk about shame and decency I've missed one thing. I don't feel ridiculous when confronted with emotional or physical nakedness, or with a sexuality that is objectively so unsuccessful. Absurdly enough, I find it far harder to acknowledge that I am generally a happy person – I feel like I'm showing off, or that I must be unaware or ignorant. I do not empathize with a world that wears people down. The prevailing aura of doom, solidarity or false modesty has brought about a similar paradox, and that sometimes makes me angry.

If I've been talking throughout this book about my Olvidado Rey Gudú incantation against sex as something that necessarily equals happiness – or maybe satisfaction would be a better way of putting it – though there's also space for sadness in my life, I identify more with Obelix when he fell in Panoramix's pothole as a child; just like Obelix when everyone else is taking the magic potion before battle, I feel a very specific sense of exclusion every time sex comes up. The main payoff? Falling in the pothole also immunized me against a sense of danger. The idea that everything will turn out alright, the daily proof that you can bear anything (within a strictly non-tragic scale, obviously) has dulled the sense of risk. By Tutatis!

Clara, in the loveliest letter I've ever received, said something I should be ashamed to repeat because it's so flattering, but I think it serves my argument here and, as well, it also happens to be true. She quoted Truman Capote's well known phrase: "when God hands you a gift, he also hands you a whip; and the whip is intended for self-flagellation". Clara said I was the exception that proved the rule. That I had turned the whip around and put on a Liza Minelli mask instead (as I did in Rome to protest the chauvinism and homophobia of its citizens, who had hassled me so much for a year). Certainly I'm one of those people who reaches the finishing line enjoying the challenge, the process of overcoming, but I'm also someone who takes time to enjoy the view, having nice chats, relishing having got there, someone who can be overcome seeing the sunrise from the bridge. But the cracks in this unruffled enjoyment began to open. It's New Year's Eve, 2010, and we start to get to the heart of the question. My faith in life and in myself has subtly also made me very controlling and on this particular December 31st, as well as desiring desire (my resolution was that this be the year of sex), I added one small clause: I wanted to let things be. My friends wouldn't believe this coming from me, from someone who two months earlier had gone to Brussels just to see a guy, someone who loved it when he was in Los Angeles and found a very messy situation there that many would have found deeply unpleasant, boyfriend included. But yes, there is a kind of straightjacket in all of this.

Looking to carry through my resolution, I went as far away as I possibly could, to New Zealand, and agreed with my friend Maruxa, one of my traveling companions, that we'd be open to anything that came our way, any sport or dangerous activity that presented itself. Risk – the magic, ignored word. And so the day of the bungee jump came. Though I of course felt shit-scared as I approached the bridge, when I got there, put the harness on, heard the attendants say one, two, three... I jumped without thinking about it. Three or four seconds later I was already at the bottom and, after a couple of bounces, came out of it cool as you like. It hadn't affected me that much because, it's true, the thought hadn't occurred to of injuring myself like Javier Bardem in The Sea Inside. I didn't consider the possibility of the safety measures failing, nor am I one of those people who doubt, peering over the edge before throwing themselves off, prolonging the moment of panic that becomes a hugely liberating feeling as soon as you jump into the abyss. I'm confident and obedient. And when the people who picked me up in the boat below asked how was it, I said "not all that." The girl said something to me along the lines of "you need your head checked".

Without risk, without chaos, without letting go of one's usual roles, is it really possible to enjoy sex fully? Though in this year of sexual mayhem, of gym shower encounters and dandy-bears, everything arose out of me asking for and getting what I want, and that is still calculated behavior, rationally formulating what one lacks and acting accordingly. This came to a head when I resolved to have a year of frivolity, which meant there was no way I could take anything seriously from then on, or when I said that I wanted to go to L.A and then four months later the editor on the World News desk was ringing me offering me exactly that (with certain provisos that, nonetheless, led me to turn down the offer). Staying with Capote: "More tears are shed over answered prayers than unanswered ones." But won't I really just be formulating my own?

I'm going to swallow my words about what I've said to do with sex not revealing anything about me, about it not being a driving factor in my life. I think that my nonaccess to it is part of my essence to the extent that it might even be my defining characteristic: my gift and my whip. Are we looking at the first ever case of "asexual obsession"? I've sometimes had the feeling of creating an absurd, antithetical kind of sexual tension that generates in the other the attraction of uncertainty. A graphic example is that I've been assaulted in the middle of the night by three different people with whom I was sharing a bed and whom I ought to curse with all the energy an asexual violator can conjure. The three of them – two of whom had boyfriends, one of whom was heterosexual – swore these were acts of somnambulism. A psychoanalyst ought to come and judge what's going on in their subconscious minds! Only one of these occasions ended up in consensual, "not-oneiric" sex. Like every time someone's cheated on their partner with me, the thought "I really don't know if the crappy sex we'll surely have will be worth it for them" occurred to me. But now that I've begun putting twos and twos together – angels and humans – innate and acquired – private and public – closets and not closets – between all of these, what can I say is inside, and what outside of me? Is sex an imposition, is it of my own making, or does it constitute a corruption of my self, a rejection of my nature? Is it simply that sex isn't for me and I have to accept it, or must these floodgates be opened and the beasts allowed to spring forth? My brother's advice for enjoying sex was: "whatever makes you go wildest is good." But what does "animal" mean in this context? Not thinking? Letting your impulses take over? Or not being a man?

I have a hard time working out whether sex takes me outside of myself and that's what stops me from enjoying it like everyone else or whether I've just never managed to let go of myself. If I have privacy back to front, my interior self on full show the whole time, then the confusion between inside and outside makes sense. Which will be why voyeurism and sex in public are the things that have turned me on most. To enter into other people's privacy or take mine out into a place where a stranger might discover it. "The whole business of eroticism is to destroy the self-contained character of the participators as they are in their normal lives... I said that I regarded eroticism as thedisequilibrium in which the being consciously calls his own existence in question. In one sense, the being loses himself deliberately, but then the subject is identified with the object losing his identity. If necessary I can say in eroticism: I am losing myself." This is how Bataille puts it.

I find it really difficult to let go of myself. The only time I experience it is in terms of artistic creation, within which I'm able to feel that the highest praise might be appropriate, as well as the most savage criticism. But this isn't the case with love, for all that there's no accounting for taste, and a person will want what they want regardless of what people say. My friend Toni, the one who said I had a problem with intimacy, "accused" me once of being above good and evil, of considering life to be a game made for my enjoyment – but always from an aloof position. It isn't for nothing that my favorite director has always been Joseph L. Mankiewicz, a master of the seventh art and tireless seeker of perfection in cinema as something to compensate for life's imperfections.

"I'm fascinated by the idea of games and the fact we are playing so much of the time that, in the end, the game begins to play with us," he used to say. As for me, perhaps by some professional mutation, sometimes I turn my life into a version of The Honey Pot, All About Eve and Sleuth. By way of the most normal over acting. Yes, the scripts aren't as good, but something of the manipulative, trouble making spirit remains. The game in which my mood can rise above the circumstances because, really, I was just moving pieces around for fun, without knowing exactly where it will lead, and sometimes meaning that the pieces turn against me. Because in games, you might enjoy it, but there's always the possibility you might lose...

My colleague Delia explains all my bizarre love stories saying that I have the power to normalize people, to make them forget their woes, and that's very attractive. Amorous situations aside, there's this unrufflable, contagious optimism about me. What she describes as my very healthy relationship with life makes it difficult for me to meet someone like me to love. This seems to be the image I transmit: an ineradicable smile and a balm for your woes. "Boy, you heal my soul," one of my more psychopathic lovers once wrote to me, three days into our relationship (in the same message he straight up called me "stupid"), so I have to think that this idea isn't totally removed from reality... although neither can it be entirely true. One last paradox: I suffer from a state of deep frivolity, not the kind of frivolity that means you enjoy a film like Legally Blonde (which I love, by the way), but in a far more radical sense. When all is said and done, I decide I how I feel – narcissistic as it might sound, I find this a comfort Everyone else, yes, goes by a little washes over me somewhat, I feel playful toward it all. Which makes me a great friend to have when people are going through difficulties – I can create a nice environment, I'm able to help people escape the tragedies drowning them. But it also makes means that I'm terrible at sharing people's lows, though I know very well how I should behave in those cases, and I have indeed put considerable work into becoming more empathic. And I've nonetheless spoken about the difference between genius and having to try – Amadeus.

In some way, given that I am always me, everything else diminishes in importance, becomes relative. Nothing threatens me because I'm in my own home, out of harm's way. What I like can't hurt me, and I do like myself. And everything fills with contradiction: since everything is mine and I am everything, what's mine is also everyone else's, as far as I'm a generous person. If my spirit is contagious, we're doing fine. Very much the Leo, it seems. Since I'm always with myself, I'm never alone, nor do I ever cease to feel like a foreigner, and that makes me an impenitent Willy Fog but eternally provincial all at once. It's my own world I'm always visiting. A very well-made world, roomy and interesting, really. But though people see me as a man of the world, really, when all is said and done, I've never made it any further than myself.

And I don't find this threatening. Not even when I had an operation on my jaw, which drew a lot of blood and left me out cold for 30 hours and my face like Elephant Man, not even then did I forsake my deep sense of calm. While all around me were losing their heads, I thought: "Take it easy, I'm still myself deep down, the same as I ever was." Mateo, the impotent almighty – endlessly hopeful about reducing tragedy, perfectly in control of self-parody and always aware in advance of his imperfections. Even though my face was a total mess after the operation, in that particular moment I met someone who later said "I fell for you the moment I laid eyes on you." But I also didn't have the patience to allow that boy to overcome his block and really be himself, which could have been so magnificent. Mateo the impatient. He who converts his life into a series of pleasurable moments but, oh, no space for sex, no, because that's when the other gets to have a say, that's when Mateo would have to leave the comfort of his world, the closet that he doesn't know if he's capable of even opening.

This mood, which can afford the illusion of a granite fortress and impregnable security (the illusion is so real that it eventually ends up playing with and even dominating me), once more becomes incompatible with intangible excitement. If I was immature through excess of maturity, if my main desire is to feel desire, now we come to the fear I feel at the thought of not feeling fear. And at being so rational, which has perhaps turned me into an unthinking animal. At the risk of overusing him, I go back to Bataille again: "Animal sexuality does make for disequilibrium and this disequilibrium is a threat to life, but the animal does not know that. Nothing resembling a question takes shape within it."

I have a lot of people who question me, but I don't doubt myself. I've found it surprisingly difficult to doubt myself ever since I was young, when I asked my cousin if she was sure that her surname was spelled the way she was spelling it and not the way I thought it should be. As an adult, it's become so that now I find it almost impossible to cast doubt on the lifesystem I myself have fabricated in the space between my upbringing and the experiences I've had, because I've had such pleasing results inside and out (if now is the time to define these two concepts) that I don't actually know if I want to change. I want to improve, because the system isn't perfect, and there's always enjoyment to be had in progress. But everything's worked better than good up until now, including with this apparently great sacrifice of riding roughshod over sexual pleasure. How to articulate this turn, then? How many renunciations does it imply? Will they make up for it all? Or am I beginning to see that this perfection crumbles precisely so that sex might be excluded from the contract?

Bataille says: "Man achieves his inner experience at the instant when bursting out of the chrysalis he feels that he is tearing himself, not tearing something outside that resists him. He goes beyond the objective awareness bounded by the walls of the chrysalis and this process, too, is linked with the turning topsy-turvy of his original mode of being." My modus operandi has negated just such a transformation. But is this now the chrysalis moment? Time for the metamorphosis? I repeat, I'm someone who enjoys not just crossing the finishing line, but the getting there too. I like positive, stable sensations, not torment and dissatisfaction. Again: happiness is far more complex than unawareness. Does this condemn me to asexuality? Or, if it is the other way around, will the emergence of a delayed sexuality bring with it an equally delayed premiere in disgrace? Although it might seem so, I'm a long way from being a conformist, for all that I gloat over the comfort of my own skin, which I have woven so carefully, why would I go out of myself to seek another? This I imagine to be narcissism's unchanging refrain. But also that of any work one does on oneself, sculpting – perhaps not entirely in the right direction – the features of a life that might appear and surely is privileged, but also happens to be the fruit of an incredibly sophisticated, perfectionist labor, though it might also at times flirt with self indulgence.

These arguments might lead me to be considered as an ice floe that has turned all around it into an immense freezer – nothing will ever melt. But it's quite the reverse: being unruffable brings one into symbiosis with letting go, because you feel as though you can wrestle with it without even messing up your hair. My world allows excessiveness, errors and mistakes, because none of that even upsets it. It's great problem is, to get to a point of surpassing its limits, one has to go a very long way, to a place of the most absolute excess. To a place where very few can follow, a place reeking of catastrophe. To get there probably signifies self-destruction. It's where the angel falls.

Niels is probably the only one who's been able to bring me anywhere near these limits, to take me to the outer reaches of what I can possibly do. And that was when, scandalized by my capacity not to collapse in the face of all his intrigues, his accusations, his bombardment of my stability (though he never knew, he came very, very close), he went nuts in the face of this haggard resistance. He tried to provoke reactions in me that never came. All he found was my certainty that, in spite of all the sorrow he was determined to find, I knew that I loved him and he loved me. His last blow against me was to say that he realized he had never loved me, and he'd never have any doubts over leaving me. It was a lie, full stop. It was as clear as day. "You're a force of nature and I can't carry on at this pace," he said in one of the few moments when he let his guard down, let his humility show. Maybe that was why he acted the victim after we broke up. Because he wasn't exactly leaving me. He was withdrawing and hoping, hopelessly, to be dissuaded. Seeing that that didn't work either, he decided if he couldn't play a part in my happiness (though in fact that was precisely what he had been), he'd play a part in my misfortune. That was why he set out to destroy me, even if it meant immolating himself. Somewhat in the manner of Gene Tierney in Leave Her to Heaven.

Indestructible, but also very destructive. In the depths of my being, the real defeat, because in reality I don't like to compete, was that I wasn't even aware that I was taking part in a contest. I was lost in my inner peace. I loved Niels deeply, with all his good and his bad points. Bad points that led me to put up with things that, from an objective standpoint, I'd always said I wouldn't put up with. But it wasn't that I didn't see them and they went unnoticed. I saw them very clearly and I was totally aware of the pain they brought about, but still wanted to be with him. I felt strong enough to carry on on foot, in spite of his blows. I was in love but hadn't lost my bearings.

For his part, Niels spent a long time idolizing everything to do with me. I idolized him, but if he did something I didn't like, and then asked me about it, I wasn't able to pretend that it was great. "Wonderful, sweetie." I carried on being unable to come out of myself. I knew Niels was my favorite person and therefore was over the moon to have met him, to look after him and give him the best of me. And to take the unfiltered gush from him, like a twenty meter-high oilstrike gushing for months and months.

For me it was perfect, but I knew it wasn't perfect in myself, because no one is. I know he thought the same of me and wanted to feel met. And once again, I showed that I don't know how to lie, and the thing I'd always held to be a virtue showed it's ugly side; one person's self assurance can, in whatever situations, morph into the support you feel knowing that someone lives under the illusion that you're the greatest. Like what my mother continues to believe about me and I see every day in her eyes. Like I should be if I one day want to have children.

What's this paradox of being so inside myself that only I can be objective? When I make a family, then I really will set myself the ultimatum of going beyond myself and leaving behind this unchangeable world I've been in up until now. I think that if there is any instinct more animal than the sexual, it's the paternal – that of wanting to protect your pack. And if I mess that up, I'll condemn my children to eternal uncertainties. And so, one way or another, my inner harmony will break down and frustration will enter my thoughts, even though a part of me will know that, in family relationships, I can always resort to overstatement. Maybe them being blood of my blood will make it less difficult. They're still within.

# GENERATIONAL SATURATION

Following this foray into the depths of individual responsibility, I now feel more at liberty to say that a society like our present one – in which sex is everywhere – doesn't much help either. It should already be clear that my hope is not to be so special as to navigate these waters alone and, while not wanting to apply the idea of "misery loves company", I don't think a certain generational logic (as I like to call it) has helped me much either.

When my mother took me to the child psychologist who, as well as exulting at my success in the intelligence test, also made one alarming comment: my mother would have to take special care with me because I was hypersensitive. Throughout my life I've monitored this hypersensitivity diagnosis thing and have found, clearly, that it isn't what my mother understood it to be – I don't in fact think it was a diagnosis at all. But it's always been on the tip of my mother's tongue as something to halt my tendency to put up barriers. I'd bet my life that when I told her I was gay her first thought was: "now I understand what this hypersensitivity thing is." Nonetheless I think my hypersensitivity had more of a key role in my second coming out and at times I see myself as the product of a series of modern patterns of scattering and saturation that, though peculiarly harmful in my case, instead of avoiding I've dived into head first.

Scattering and saturation have found their perfect breeding ground in the marvelous invention known as the internet, something I consider to mark a turning point that will be studied in the future as the beginning of a new historical era. Not 9/11, not Obama, not the fall of the Berlin Wall. I'm hardly the first to point out that the Information Age will be considered a real agent of change in the world's habits and customs.

Above and beyond the pace of everything, global connectedness and online shopping, I'm hardly saying anything particularly dazzling or new if I point out that our ways of thinking have also been changed. Here I'm appropriating a point made by a friend of mine and I believe these panes named Windows, as well as the subdividable tabs within them so you can toggle between webpages in record time, have made us accustomed to keeping various fronts open at once. How often do we find ourselves with a page up and not know exactly what we're looking at or what's led us there? Utterly the same sensation as when we find ourselves in the kitchen but forget what it was we came to get. But online, this scattering tendency is proliferated. And in the fields of sex and emotion, depending on your point of view, in chatrooms and, as far as I know, gay ones especially, it reigns supreme. To be specific, since smartphones have been around, we're talking pretty much about something pathological.

Full disclosure: the internet has been a crucial exploratory weapon, emotional and sexual, in my desire hunt. In my view the gay world has been streets ahead of the heterosexual for years – though they're starting to becoming more equal now. And for anyone not familiar with the universe I'm speaking about, I can assure them that it features as much bad as good. Just like life. Careful of the procedures, though; they make all the difference. Every one of these sites are like the same dog but with a different collar – GayRomeo, Gaydar, ManHunt, Bear, Bakala, to name but a few – the idea being that each will be more or less appropriate to different kinds of people – more romantic, more international, more sexual, more bear, more masculine, respectively – but the users are the same on each, people who have all five open at once and are sending and receiving messages constantly. I don't come at this judgmentally, not at all – I use said sites. It isn't hard to tell.

If on the one hand I'll always argue the case for internet users as autonomous entities and I believe that in what is supposedly a virtual sphere, real sensations of excitement and delight intersect on them, when it comes to the face to face moment (I hesitate to call it the moment of truth, though so many do), most likely your mind is on the cards that are still to be revealed. On the string of options, of possible other men you've thought about going for coffee with one day – and seeing what it leads to... Which itself leads to the feeling that, in the not hugely likely case that attraction arises live and direct, and starts going somewhere, there will always be the bitter aftertaste of not having gone with any of the other men it could have been. You often want to do the same as when you're shopping and say, I'm going to have more of a look around, and I might be back. Some do exactly that, in fact. But it does mean you can end up spending most of the time trying on shoes that look awful. And ones that jab into you. Plus the obvious fact that when you come back to the ones you liked, someone will probably have gone off with them.

This commercialization of relations – this search, compare and if you don't find anything better, buy – doesn't only apply to sex. I'm amongst those who believe gay chatrooms will do away with gay prostitution (because, really, online, where there's a will there's a way – plus it's free), but in the field of emotions, as well, the level of intimacy you can get to on a first date is also dizzying. On first dates I've found myself relating my whole life story, the complete works, and had exactly the same from my interlocutor. When you came out – whether your parents know or not – what emotional baggage you're carrying, what thoughts of fidelity, of commitment... Female friends tell me that people feel relaxed around me, but the truth of it is that people want to uncover as quickly as possible whatever it is that will mean it won't work. The acid test, version 2.0. The most worrying thing is that you start to feel that the two involved are more keen to seek out stains than immaculate whites. Rejection feels like more of a relief than success. Strange.

Sex – there it is – yours if you want it. At the push of a button. And in I rush – ever since I was tiny, danger always called to me and I'd end up falling into the ravine. I struggle having so many doubts and no solutions. Or receiving messages containing propositions and saying no to all of them. Some pique my curiosity. Assertiveness, Mateo, assertiveness. A lot of people mess about endlessly, never dare make the leap. Fantasize a little, get horny with whoever and, blatantly, jerk off all alone, and are more than happy. Nor do I see this as wrong. When it comes to this online way of doing things, everyone enjoys the upsides, but also swallows the drawbacks.

But I believe that this sexual omnipresence, which extends to society in general, to marketing, cinema, to the watercooler… everywhere, is actually to our detriment. Or mine at least. I'm not going to get all nostalgic for a past I wasn't alive to experience, or glorify censorship as something that forced such elaborate pathways that proceedings were always passionate and sex a tremendous release. But sex becoming nothing more than money has ultimately led to a loss of interest.

"The best way of enlarging and multiplying one's desires is to try to limit them," said the Marquis de Sade. Well, if we already have no limits, we're going to have to multiply by zero. But its economic equation is quite unlike any other: there has been so much speculation that prices have gone down rather than up. We can now talk of sexual inflation. But at the same time of an absolute devaluation. Nowadays no one would bat an eyelid at Madonna. Which is why people like her less and less… and I carry on liking her. In a way, a bubble has been created in sex like it was in the property market: everyone's jumped on board in trying to accumulate and accumulate different kinds of sex. On the beach and in the mountains, for when you're on holiday or for the day to day. They can't get enough. Sale ends soon. Absolute bargain. On the internet you can create your own search criteria preferences to the point that there's even a way to find tourists in your city, for the ones who will never ask you to explain. Someone says what they're looking for and believes they've found it even though, much as I think the internet tends to make people more honest, deceitful publicity is seriously also on the menu.

With this "democratization" of sex and with everyone fucking everyone (gays at least, making full use of the internet and chowing down whenever they can), the protocol have been lost – at the risk of sounding old-fashioned and a bit obvious – the normal rules of seduction have been lost. Objective criteria have been confused with this intangible membrane – physical skin – that marks the point between others, the difference, and makes someone attractive to you though you have no idea why. We end up looking amongst pseudotribes of people who are seeking or offering the same, forgetting the fact that the best thing about a partner is that they refresh you and upset your schema precisely by dint of being so different from you. We forget about the rebellious difference between a desire for excellence and a desire for others – that what you desire is quite different to what you think you desire. And when you add some conquest or other on Facebook, looking at how many "friends" you have in common on that particular social network, you see there's any number: the guy you struck up a conversation with yesterday, the one you went out with last week, the one you were sleeping with at Christmas. Then, if you start rummaging around in the photo albums of friends of friends, you start seeing photos you recognize, of people you only knew before by nickname online, but now all of a sudden you can see first name, last name and what they do for a living. Welcome: you left the Pyrenees of Aragon in search of world of opportunities and all you've really ended up with is another village, all the more homogenous. At least when you were at school you found yourself alongside the baker's son, the dirty capitalist and a couple of gypsies who never made it past fourth grade. Now the biggest difference you're likely to come across is someone saying they liking Antonioni more than Bergman. But there we are... couple of tabs open (not Bakala or ManHunt, not for me, sorry) just checking things out, just in case, having a little look when I find myself bored or on going somewhere on a train.

And then it's also true that I've met really lovely people, which still seems to me, with my appetite for the social, something verifiably useful. But it doesn't take long to reach saturation point, and the web is jammed with profiles saying "back again" – we've all had that sudden feeling of wanting to delete our accounts and go back to picking people up in the street, to daring to ask for a phone number, pretending we've dropped something, to drop in silly references – all of which quickly takes back on its extraordinary allure.

Though virtual, there's something orgiastic in this milieu. But not like people being scandalous just to be provocative – to which I feel immune – but as something that's counterproductive. "The orgy is necessarily disappointing. Theoretically it is the complete negation of the individual quality. It presupposes, it even demands equality among the participants. Not only is individuality itself submerged in the tumult of the orgy, but each participant denies the individuality of the others. All limits are completely done away with, or so it seems, but it is impossible for nothing to remain of the differences between individuals and the sexual attraction connected to those differences," said Bataille. And there, right there, that's where I find myself now. Trapped in a collective that I feel is swallowing my individuality up.

Within this diluted individuality, this devoured scattering, I feel that I, who loved both so much, have finally come to feel less concerned with myself. Because when I put the brakes on, stop the whole frenetic machine and am alone, I realize I I haven't been aware of myself for a long while – and then sometimes I don't recognize myself. It makes my relationship with myself something like that between a divorced father and his children: he sees them so rarely that when his weekend with them finally comes around, he doesn't go into anything deep with them but just buys them their favorite ice creams to keep them happy, enjoying a nice bit of relaxation, a bit of a time out from the crisis. And then I'm reminded of close friends who have decided to go and live together and one day, without having realized, see that, since it's a given they'll see each other at home, don't make plans to go out any more and their interaction has reduced to little more than good morning and good night. Compared to what my selves once were, look at us now: devoured by routine and slovenliness. And this saddens me, because I'm not a person to run from myself or to not face up to problems. But faced with such a range of options, it isn't that you become a more eclectic person, but you find paths to authenticity that are both convincing and incompatible, one eclipsing the other if a little order isn't introduced. In the same way that, though I like eating at home as much as going out for dinner, I always end up taking the less healthy, more expensive option, a characteristic I so value in myself – introspection – has drowned in the well of hypersociability. The outside always trumps the inside. Which is why, in the gallery of appealing and shiny things, sex has also been overlooked – now that it isn't something transgressive, but something routine. Any old flat mate to just say hey to, automatically, and with whom the formalities have become far too lax. After having taken years to understand it as something altogether extraordinary in my life, I've shifted without noticing to apathy and, what's worse, bashfulness. My fault, of course, because no one makes me act like this... Or do they?

Asexuals, when demanding recognition as a collective on AVEN, acknowledge that they aren't an oppressed collective in the conventional sense, because of the fact that for all someone says "I confess", you can never be as damned for omission as for words and deeds. Asexuals are not forced into doing anything concrete, nor are they incarcerated for their non-practise – for all that people do consider them aberrant. No rehab or reintegration therapies exist for this (imagine!). It's quite something else, for example, to force myself of my own accord to do something that is at no one else's bequest. But being ignored or ostracized in this way generates a certain discomfort, because it condemns the collective to pass by relatively unnoticed, and there's something very painful about that.

October 14, 2004, an article in New Scientist by Sylvia Pagan Westphal appeared to shed light on this, speaking as it did about the possible beginnings of an asexual revolution. For a number of months it "trended high", as we'd say nowadays. On AVEN, seventy or so members would go online every day, including David Jay, the interviewee in that article, and the forum became animated, people commented and discussed... Dr. Bogaert published his study, drawn to the surface by the heat generated by the discussion among the most radical part of the movement, those people who had neither had nor wanted to have sexual relations. But like every news story, the thing deflated when the media outlets decided that the story had run its course. A shame, because it also failed to break out of the U.S, it certianly never got much airplay in Spain. Did anyone have any idea about this in Spain? I obviously didn't. So that when I wrote the article, to the best of my modest abilities, it came as something fairly new to everyone close to me... and it didn't stoke up any response other than the usual "Mateo's on about his weird shit again."

Modern society, as I've said now a few times, has loaded sex with a sense of obligation. As someone once said, in the past you were judged for what you did, and nowadays you're judged by what you don't. Sex has become such a pressure, such a millstone.

"Since time immemorial, and probably in all cultures, sexuality has been governed by systems of constraint; but it is a comparatively recent particularity of our own culture to have divided it so rigorously into Reason and Unreason. As a consequence and degradation of that, it was not long before it was also classified into healthy or sick, normal or abnormal," wrote Foucault. I've been making the case for an un-undressing for ages, how hard it is to find balance, a midway point. If only Aristotle would come and lend a hand.

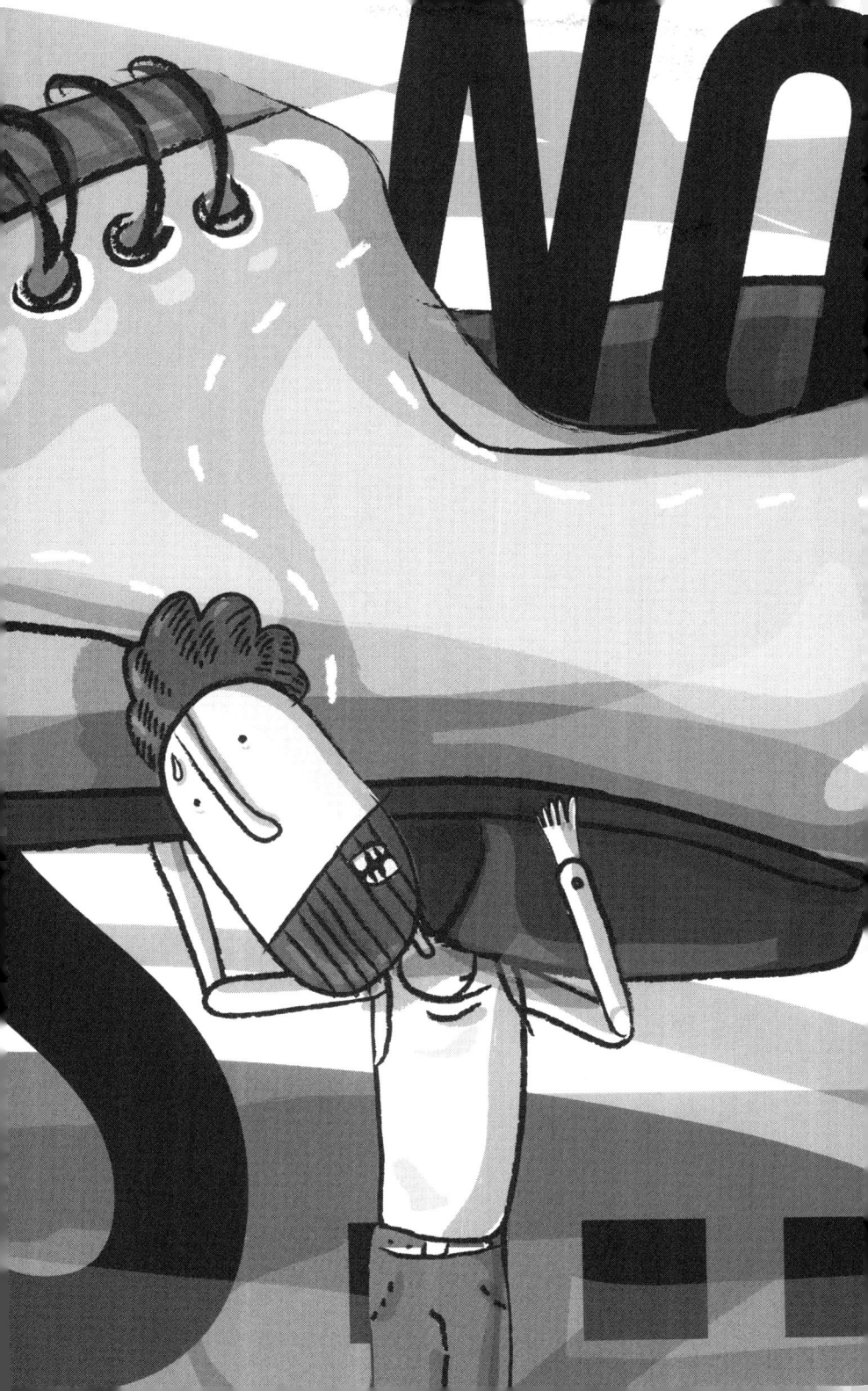

# HIS AND HERS

With this whole desire mess splashed all over the floors now, all that remains for me to discuss are the women I've crossed paths with in my life and that, amongst all the asexualization, have found cracks to poke around in. I'm not only talking about those pregay adolescence amours, which were flushed, immaculate, Platonic and altogether lovely, but rather the women that once I had come to terms with my homosexuality made me feel that my closet had revolving doors like luxury hotel entrances.

Once, dressed up as Liza Minnelli (I got that particular outfit down to a tee) I got into a thing with a girl who turned out to be my flatmate's brother's girlfriend (a guy who I've also always thought was hot). All those fish in the sea and I end up with this one! But anyway: going around dressed up as a woman can be considered as a homosexual experience and, in fact, her boyfriend thought: "That's Mateo to a tee". Sometimes reality is so unreal...

At a festival in San Sebastian, a girl I'd been talking to about musicals, about dance and others such highly macho subjects, starting giving me the eye, and came out with it: she liked me. We ended up kissing passionately, to the annoyance of all my straight friends, who all went home furious. There was far more of an emotional charge that day, and I now see that I felt really bad. Strangely, having had lots of purely functional relations with men, I didn't feel the same with this particular woman. Will I look down on women too, assume they're the weaker sex, emotionally insufficient? Or was I just conscious of the farce involved?

In Rome, which for me was what jail would be for a straight guy, I went off on a tangent (but a good one) and fell for a woman. To start with we had your typical gay-best friend relationship. But a moment came when physical contact became so intense that I began to experience a lot of doubt. She left and I felt a tremendous absence. I cried like I've never cried for a man and, the next year, when I went to Helsinki on an internship, I decided to change tack when I heard that she was going to Madrid. I wanted to find out what it was between us exactly and take the bull by the horns.

The situation started becoming more normal, basically because I arrived from Rome and, now I remember, lost my virginity; for all that I'd long since come to terms with my homosexuality, I'd had a couple of long amours that had nonetheless left "my flower" intact – like a boy who wouldn't do it without a lifelong promise. When it happened, the experience was neither traumatic nor untraumatic, but I fell helplessly in love with the guy, who was in Seville and who, though he later on turned out to be leading me on, ticked perfectly all the boxes when it came to dynamism, stimulation, intelligence, attraction and fun – I was head over heels. But something in me always drew me back to the story with this girl: there was always some kind of compatibility between my love for other guys and my love for her. A complementarity, even. As if I were a swimmer, sometimes doing backstroke, sometimes front crawl; each activated different emotional muscles in me.

This girl acted in such a way that, even if the norm, I still found startling: she felt she could grope her little gay friend unceremoniously whenever she felt like it. I've had the same thing from other women and it isn't that I don't like it – quite the opposite – but it's still surprising. I suppose the rules of this particular game have something to do with the fact they can cease to worry about making a guy horny with the merest brush, they can let themselves get carried away knowing it won't excite us or make us feel uncomfortable. A sweet – not hard – affection; relaxed – everything flaccid. I remember the looks I got from a guy who was on an Erasmus year when he saw as many as five girls milling around me, cuddling and tickling, playing with my hair... "Bastard! I'm going to start saying I'm gay too!" But how excited can a woman get with what, after all, is a man whom their touching totally indiscreetly? I imagine myself taking the opposite role, with a straight guy whom I'm certain I won't arouse, and precisely because of that I try my hardest, fondling, a little bit more even... and I don't know what to say. Working from the certainty that, like one of these abandoned dogs posters, his mental schematic would dictate that he'd never do it. But I also think that for my part I wouldn't be being entirely fraternal...

The thing is that we were always very tactile with each other, and this began to get a little out of hand. Or at least I started to get a bit anxious, with the maelstrom I had going on inside me. As is my way, I decided to speak openly about it. She was super taken aback, obviously. "I've always thought of you as gay," she said, struck by the obviousness of what she was saying. Obviously. In that moment I couldn't have cared less about the proper ways of conducting one self. I think it was one of the few times in my life when I've felt genuinely downcast. What a mess! I'll always ask myself how far she and I might have gone together or what the difference would have been between being with a guy because of the sex I only like having in small doses or with her with whom the sex, in principle, never occurred to me. Splitting hairs, I know.

But this brings me to another of the asexual's conflicts that has already been put forward: why don't we take advantage of the fact that sex doesn't get us going and learn to use it in a more utilitarian way? Which is to say: why, given that I'm not going to enjoy it as much, don't I just have sex with a women and thereby access something that is a strong desire in me – having children? The answer is actually straightforward, clear and resounding: out of respect for the woman in question. But when it came to this woman I'm talking about, my schema shifted, I mean I felt I was making my way through unsettling terrain, yes, but, undoubtedly, through the authentic too. With the taboo feeling that had been there for a few months now placated, and feeling reconciled to the fact that we cohabit marvelously well, which made for a lovely summer together in San Francisco in which everything was smooth as silk, the idea of dividing things up returned and loomed over me: and if this is the family model I want for my future? In times when she hadn't had a boyfriend she saw it as clearly as I did but, logically enough, the rejection for a heterosexual woman is much greater in these cases, because she's able have a child with the person she's in love with if that's what comes up. And, deep down, my relationship with this girl is an almost exact copy of the one I had or could have had with Alfonso. That's the way things are.

Then, as much as with her as with him, there is an imperative that signals to you that this situation is a pressure cooker. I don't know if it's that you withdraw in search of a internal coherence that dictates to you better than anyone what you ought to do or, maybe, what overwhelms you is a fear of complexity and the maturity implied by these new ways of relating to people. Success is clearly never guaranteed, not even in apparently model emotional relationships – every emotion is wont to swerve in unexpected directions. But why do we feel more secure clothed in classical or already tried and tested structures? Centuries of social evolution must, I imagine, create an illusion of solidity. Therefore I get lost between cowardice and realism. And when I see AVEN's David Jay talking about amorous triangulations, of becoming a "bonus" for a couple and exchanging sex for something Zen, I say to myself: Mateo, you're simply not cut out for these new fangled ways. You're a straightforward guy, raised according to the best values of respect and empathy, both of which this whole mess threatens to do away with. But don't worry: remember that everything usually turns out pretty well for you.

What do we do with the new structures then? For me, on one side they cause me a lot of stress, which isn't especially worrying, but also a lot of confusion, which is worse. What exactly did I feel for that girl? There are so many theories... from the Kinsey scale – which might put me at 4 for homosexuality and 2 for heterosexuality – to the idea that my sex counselor friend had about people who are sexually ambiguous: he just said you have to be open to everything because the categories don't really cover everything. But on the other side, Clara, somewhat more grounded, says I like this girl because she's resembles my mother more than any of my other female friends, ergo she brings out my frustration with the impossibility of forming a traditional family. Not, N.B, as a rejection of homosexuality in itself, but an obvious impotence around how tricky it is to create a stable home: via adoption, which is economically tricky, via mothers for rent (apologies to anyone who finds that a dated phrase), which is morally tricky, or via having a child with a friend which I would imagine leading to seeing the child only on holidays, like a niece or nephew.

But then again, who would deny the feeling I had for her? I don't believe that projections that strong exist or, if they do exist, I think if they are so very strong, that then makes them valid. Anyway, what feeling doesn't begin in a needing, a wanting, or some kind of complex? If we have to scrap every one of our distinguishing features because we consider them products of our relationship with our environment, I think we'd diminish ourselves to essentially squalid entities, pierced by variously poorly managed excuses. And that truly would be a bullshit way to be.

But then I go back to my argument that, in spite of sexuality's social lining, no one will ever banish sex altogether given that it's the very essence of being. My siblings' beings, having been raised the same as me. In those of my peers, who are subjected to the same bombardment of stimuli as me. Sex, if it's innate, will always go on and it is, yes, it is, beyond good and evil. That's nature, and like nature, it can't be fought against. To quote Foucault one last time: "Things and words were to be separated from one another. The eye was thenceforth destined to see and only to see, the ear to hear and only to hear. The prose of the world was still to have the task of speaking that which is, but it was no longer to be anything more than what it said." Maybe this will all just be an absurd rhetorical exercise in which, trying to attain epic proportions, I'd like to think that after years of analyzing the relationship between Eros and Thanatos, and treatises on the relationship between sex and death, it has never occurred to anyone that someone might kill their own sex. And then I came along. Such a dubious pioneer.

Even though I see myself at a pivotal moment, the pivot creaks: plagued by possibilities but still hooked on the same models as ever. A conflict very well depicted in the frivolous and heartbreaking film Beloved featuring Catherine Deneuve and Chiara Mastroianni, directed by Christophe Honoré and which closed Cannes in 2011. What's great about being a journalist and being there is that, if you feel it won't be too out of place, you have the chance to transfer your existential doubts to someone like Catherine Deneuve. I asked her (it was relevant at the time, I swear) if she thought that the sexualemotional uncertainty that characterizes the turn of the twenty first century had come out of the turning point we're living through or if we are condemned, with the opening up of all these wonderful possibilities, to live in confusion and in the permanent sensation of renunciation. A bit of a debate started up around the table, one of the cast, Paul Schneider, answering first, who said: "It's a great thing to have fifteen types of mustard in the supermarket," he said. "But, yes, it can also get a bit overwhelming." Fine. But then the great Deneuve spoke: "It takes two to make a couple, and they are the ones who have to be true to themselves, though that might mean, in the eyes of society, they're considered untrue." If she says so, it must be true. The only rule is that the two have to agree on the rules. Or the three, or the four.

But when I said that honesty was fundamental for us all to be much happier, I forgot one small detail: that honesty only works when one really know which is one's true interior. In those moments in which no one, me included, knows what they want, when there are thousands of mirrors and doubt everywhere as to the direction, origin and meaning of our desires, this honesty is sure to be so changeable that I struggle to believe in its worth. Are we condemned to trial and error or will clearsightedness one day be ours again? " I believe that truth has only one face: that of a violent contradiction," concluded Bataille. Right on the money, I think, once again.

With or without raging contradictions, in both the straight and gay worlds, the options are being given more attention. But what does that mean I do with the unexplored range of options in asexuality, lack of appetite or whatever this thing is that I try and at other times refuse to adjust to? For now, the only thing that's occurred to me is to write this book. After that, we'll see. Let things be.

NO
BO
DY IS
PERFECT

Made in the USA
San Bernardino, CA
23 August 2017